Spin ❀ Dye ❀ Stitch

❋ How to Create and Use Your Own Yarns ❋

Jennifer Claydon

NORTH LIGHT BOOKS
Cincinnati, Ohio

www.mycraftivity.com

13   12   11   10   09   5   4   3   2   1

Distributed in Canada by Fraser Direct
100 Armstrong Avenue
Georgetown, ON, Canada L7G 5S4
Tel: (905) 877-4411

Distributed in the U.K. and Europe by David & Charles
Brunel House, Newton Abbot, Devon, TQ12 4PU, England
Tel: (+44) 1626 323200, Fax: (+44) 1626 323319
E-mail: postmaster@davidandcharles.co.uk

Distributed in Australia by Capricorn Link
P.O. Box 704, S. Windsor, NSW 2756 Australia
Tel: (02) 4577-3555

Library of Congress Cataloging-in-Publication Data
Claydon, Jennifer.
  Spin, dye, stitch : how to create and use your own yarns
/ Jennifer Claydon. -- 1st ed.
      p. cm.
  Includes index.
  ISBN 978-1-60061-155-1 (pbk. : alk. paper)
 1. Hand spinning. 2. Dyes and dyeing, Domestic. 3.
Yarn. I. Title.
  TT847.C54 2009
  746.1'2--dc22
                                                2009001529

EDITORS: Jessica Gordon and Julie Hollyday

DESIGNER: Geoff Raker

PHOTOGRAPHERS: Christine Polomsky and Ric Deliantoni

STYLIST: Jan Nickum

PRODUCTION COORDINATOR: Greg Nock

TECHNICAL EDITOR: Amy Polcyn

fw
media
www.fwmedia.com

Dedication

To Betty Claydon, my mom. Mom, thank you for your life-long support of my dreams; for being an amazing mom; for being an even more amazing friend; and for being an example of the kind of woman I hope to be. Your kindness, compassion, courage and strength are a lot to live up to, but I sure will try.

To Mark Hale, my boyfriend when I started this book, now my fiancé, and soon to be my husband. Thank you for your love, your friendship, your constant support, your staunch belief that spinning is cool, and, of course, all the laughs and baked goods you provided during the writing of this book. I would have been ten times as crazy without you.

I love you both with all my heart, and this book, like everything I do that is good, is dedicated to both of you.

Metric Conversion Chart

to convert	to	multiply by
Inches	Centimeters	2.54
Centimeters	Inches	0.4
Feet	Centimeters	30.5
Centimeters	Feet	0.03
Yards	Meters	0.9
Meters	Yards	1.1
Sq. Inches	Sq. Centimeters	6.45
Sq. Centimeters	Sq. Inches	0.16
Sq. Feet	Sq. Meters	0.09
Sq. Meters	Sq. Feet	10.8
Sq. Yards	Sq. Meters	0.8
Sq. Meters	Sq. Yards	1.2
Pounds	Kilograms	0.45
Kilograms	Pounds	2.2
Ounces	Grams	28.3
Grams	Ounces	0.035

About the Author

Jenni Claydon is a book editor by day, an author by night and a fiber artist at all times. Her current artistic endeavors include spinning gossamer-weight yarns that she then knits into lace shawls of her own design. Jenni lives, loves and hoards fiber in Cincinnati. Her house made of wool also contains one very understanding partner and two rambunctious cats.

Acknowledgments

Dedicating this book to Mark and my mom, Betty, just isn't enough to thank them for all they did to make this book happen. Thanks to both of them for their support, patience and understanding. And special thanks to my mom for invaluable knitting assistance. Without her that darn blanket on page 84 wouldn't exist.

I would also like to thank all the spinners who contributed to the yarn gallery at the end of this book. There is so much talent in the spinning community today, and I am honored that these generous artists shared their work with me.

Thanks to all of my coworkers at F+W, especially those who directly contributed to the making of this book, and those who taught me to be a better editor and author. It's a pleasure working with all of you. To be a little more specific:

Thanks are more than due to my editors, Jessica Gordon and Julie Hollyday. Throughout the editing process they were both supportive, cheerful and accommodating. I couldn't have done this without their help and expertise. They are an editing dream team!

Words aren't enough to teach spinning—seeing the process is key. The person behind the incredible step-by-step photographs in this book is Christine Polomsky. Christine is not just an awesome photographer and not just a great coworker—she is a wonderful friend. This book wouldn't have been possible without her talent, friendship and great laugh. Thanks as well to Ric Deliantoni and Jan Nickum, who shot and styled the beautiful photography for this book. Thank you for making everything look wonderful!

My thanks to Geoff Raker for the fantastic design work he did on this book—and for turning his kitchen into a dyeing set for our photo shoot. It was a big leap of faith on his part to believe that I wouldn't dye his lovely antique stove blue.

Last, I want to thank all the talented artists who contributed to my fiber arts education. Your teaching has proved to be a priceless gift—a source of entertainment, enjoyment, peace and more. Thank you.

Contents

Introduction 6

Introduction

Over the past few years, there has been a huge boom in the craft world. Handcrafts are being rediscovered and reinvented at an amazing rate, especially the ones involving yarn and fiber. I couldn't be happier about this trend. I have always been a die-hard crafter, and lately I've been able to bring more and more unsuspecting victims—oh, I mean new crafters—into the fold. What I like even better than the initial surge of new crafters is that the people who dove into "our" world thinking that knitting is the new yoga are beginning to drift off. They've discovered that knitting is not the new yoga; knitting is knitting (or weaving is weaving, or needle felting is needle felting—you get the idea).

The crafters who stuck around, the ones who love that knitting is knitting, are hungry for more. They want to know more about what they are making, and they want more control over the process. Many crafters are diving deeper into their art and discovering new avenues to explore. If you are one of those crafters, this book is for you.

The longer you stay in this world of yarn, fiber, knitting needles, felting needles, sewing needles, warping boards and more, the more likely you are to run into a dreaded situation: the moment when you can't find Just What You Want. For me, that time came when I couldn't find just the right silk thread for a tatting project. I had briefly stumbled into spinning when I bought a drop spindle at my local weaving supplier. That first time around, spinning didn't stick. But, after a long and arduous search for that perfect silk thread, it occurred to me that I might be able to make it myself. That was when I really fell down the rabbit hole. Four wheels, two drum carders and I can't even guess how much fiber later, it happened again. I couldn't find just the right color. Hello, dyeing.

If you have ever wondered how yarn gets made or whether you could make it yourself, you have come to the right place. You can spin and dye your way to Just What You Want. Fiber content, color, texture, thickness and more can all be under your control. I will show you how to get started with spinning and dyeing and with making your own custom yarns. After that, I will show you how to use those first lumpy, bumpy yarns in a few projects designed specifically for those first imperfect efforts. As a bonus, there is also an inspirational gallery of yarns from some very talented spinners. Inside this book is something for every crafter and every mood.

If you are in need of a quiet evening or a calm, centering activity, give spinning a whorl (sorry, bad spinner's pun). If you want to pretend to be a mad chemist, dyeing will tickle your fancy. If you want to have the deep satisfaction of really making something from beginning to end, try both dyeing and spinning. Those precious projects you plan and execute from start to finish will be worth more than their weight in gold (although you can't actually spin straw into gold, contrary to what fairy tales say).

❋ SPIN ❋

Throughout the ages, spinning has gone through many transformations. Yarn production started on spindles and then moved to spinning wheels. For thousands of years, people spun out of necessity. Every bit of thread, yarn or fabric began as raw fiber spun by hand. From thread used to stitch fine fabrics to rope used to anchor ships, a spinner's hand could be seen in all things made from fiber. During the industrial revolution, spinning became mechanized, and the advances in technology eventually took spinning out of most hands. In some cultures today, hand spinning is still a part of everyday life, but for most people spinning is a thing of the past.

However, for a small but growing community, spinning has become necessary again in a creative sense, even though it may not be necessary in an economic sense. From casual crafters to dedicated fiber artists, spinning once again has a following. And why shouldn't it? There is so much to love about spinning. Take color—from the subtle tones of nature's palette to the rainbow explosion of an indie dyer's imagination, there's something for every taste. And texture! There are springy fibers such as wool; curly ones like mohair; decadence with cashmere; and luscious textures with fibers like silk. And those are just fiber choices. Once you've picked your fiber, there are design choices to consider. You get to choose the tools, spinning method, yarn weight, number of plies and more. The creative possibilities are endless.

The act of spinning itself is also a joy. Maybe not right at the beginning—in the beginning it's like patting your head and rubbing your stomach and singing a happy little tune. But once you've got the motions down pat, once your hands learn what they need to do, it's a joy. The rhythms of hand spinning are meditative and calming, and the connection to all the spinners who came before you is almost palpable. The connections you can form with today's spinners are wonderful, too. There's nothing like a gathering of friends, fun and fiber. When you try your hand at hand spinning, you'll discover a whole new world of creativity.

Spinning Materials and Tools

To start spinning, you only need two things: something to spin and something to spin with. For thousands of years, this meant fiber and a stone on a stick (or sometimes just a stick). Fortunately, today's spinners have many more choices, and spinning materials and tools are widely available. I still suggest starting simple; some well-prepared fiber and a well-made drop spindle are all you need to make your first yarn. If you decide that spinning is for you, you can invest in more sophisticated tools to suit your spinning style.

Spinning Materials (aka Fiber)

Buying fiber for spinning is becoming easier and easier. Small quantities of fiber are available in most large craft stores now and in some local knitting and weaving shops. And all varieties of spinning fiber are now easy to find on the Internet. This is a big change from a couple decades ago when my spinning friends were so desperate to find spinnable fiber that they saved dryer lint and begged for cotton from pill bottles at pharmacies. Knowing some details about fiber will help you choose the right fiber for your spinning endeavors.

Types of Fiber

Different types of fiber are usually classified by their source. The categories spinners have to choose from are plant, animal and "other." Within these categories are further divisions. Each type of fiber has unique characteristics that influence the finished yarn. Here is some basic information about the most popular types of fiber.

Plant Fibers

Plant fibers are especially popular in warm climates where the warmth of animal fiber is unnecessary. Cotton is the most well-known plant fiber, but flax (used to make linen), ramie and hemp are also widely available. All of these plant fibers are harvested directly from the plant with minimal processing needed before they can be spun. Many more plant-based fibers are available on the market, such as bamboo, soy silk, ingeo and rayon, but these fibers are manufactured fibers, meaning they are produced through chemical processes. These chemically processed fibers do not come directly from the plant; they are produced by humans.

Synthetic Fibers

Manufactured fibers are fibers that are produced by humans. Some manufactured fibers are synthetic, such as nylon and Mylar. These fibers can be blended with natural fibers to add strength or a decorative element. Several new manufactured fibers are currently available that are protein- or cellulose-based. These fibers can be spun alone or in blends. Protein- and cellulose-based manufactured fibers are chemically produced from natural materials, such as milk, corn, soybeans or bamboo. These fibers are not natural, however. They are produced in factories through chemical processes.

Animal Fibers

Wool is fiber that has been sheared from a sheep. It is one of the most commonly used spinning fibers and a great choice for beginning spinners. The staple length of the most commonly available wools (approximately 3" to 5" [8cm to 13cm]) is ideal for a new spinner to work with, and the crimp in wool makes it easy to handle. Not all wool is created equally,

1   2   3   4   5   6   7   8

1. Medium Wool	5. Cashmere
2. Fine Wool	6. Yak
3. Llama	7. Bison
4. Camel	8. Silk

though—different breeds of sheep produce different kinds of wool. The breeds are usually classified by the fineness of the fiber they produce.

Fine wool sheep, such as Merino and Cormo, produce soft fleeces. The yarns made from these fleeces are also soft, but the fiber can sometimes be more difficult to spin because the fine fibers are also a bit slippery. Medium wool sheep, such as Corriedale and Targhee, produce the most beginner-friendly fleeces. Medium wool has enough length to work with without being too long, and the fibers aren't soft enough to be slippery, but they're not so rough that they're unpleasant to work with. Long wool sheep, including Romney and Lincoln, have coarse fleeces that also usually have quite a bit of sheen. The strength of these fibers makes them good candidates for hardwearing items such as outerwear and rugs. There are also double- or dual-coated sheep, such as Shetland and Icelandic, which have two types of fiber in their fleece; a long, coarse outer coat, and a light, soft down coat. Both types of fiber can be spun.

Other animal fibers are also commonly used for spinning. Technically, any animal hair or fur can be spun, though extremely coarse or short fibers should be avoided. Some of the most popular animal fibers today include alpaca, llama, camel, mohair, angora and cashmere. Exotic (and expensive) fibers like qiviut, guanaco, buffalo, pygora and vicuna are becoming widely available as well.

Another very popular "animal" fiber is silk, which is different from other animal fibers in that it is not hair or fur. Silk is produced by silkworms when they create a cocoon. The cocoons are boiled to separate the silk from other materials in the cocoon.

Each of these animal fibers has its own unique characteristics: Fiber length, fineness, crimp (or lack thereof), color and more vary from one fiber to another. To save yourself frustration, do a little research about a new fiber before you begin spinning it. Learning from the trials and travails of spinners who came before you will save you time and money!

Fiber Blends

Blends made from multiple fibers are also popular with spinners because the best characteristic of each fiber can be highlighted. Mixing cashmere with wool makes a blend that is easier to spin than cashmere by itself and softer than wool alone. Mixing wool with silk makes a blend with more sheen than wool alone and more loft than straight silk. Have fun and experiment with different combinations.

12

Fiber Preparation

Unfortunately, fiber does not come straight off an animal or plant ready to spin. The fiber must be prepared for spinning. This process usually includes cleaning and then arranging the fibers. Many fiber artists (including me) enjoy preparing their own fibers. However, prepared fibers are widely available and can be great time-savers. I recommend starting with prepared fibers so you can dive straight into spinning.

Combing and carding are the two overarching categories of fiber preparation. While there are divisions within each category, the most important distinction in fiber preparation is combed fiber versus carded fiber. Combing, also referred to as a worsted preparation, aligns the fibers parallel to each other and removes short fibers from the mix. Combed fibers produce the smoothest yarns. This is the most time-intensive, and therefore also the most expensive,

A Note About Fiber Qualities

Once you've been really bitten by the spinning bug, you'll start amassing a stash of spinning fibers. Besides knowing about fiber content and preparation, here are a few things you should look for when buying fiber.

Microns and Bradford count are measurements used to describe the fineness of fiber. A micron measurement tells you a single fiber's diameter. The smaller the micron count, the finer the fiber. For example, an average Merino, a fine wool, is 18 to 22 microns; and Corriedale, a medium wool, is 22 to 34 microns.

Bradford count is a classification system used to measure how many skeins of yarn could be spun from one pound of wool. The higher the Bradford count, the finer the fiber. For example, on average Merino wool has a Bradford count in the 80s to 60s and Corriedale wool has a Bradford count in the 60s to 40s.

Length, sometimes also referred to as staple length, plays a big role in how difficult or easy a fiber is to spin. Very short and very long fibers are both difficult to spin. To begin, choose fibers that are around 3½" to 5" (9cm to 13cm) long. To learn how to find a fiber's staple length, see page 23.

Crimp is a term you'll probably remember if you survived the late 1980s and early 1990s. Do you remember crimping your own hair? Many fibers have those little ripples naturally. Crimp gives a fiber stretch and bounce and also a little bit of grip to make it easier to spin. Fibers without crimp, including angora or silk, feel more slippery than fibers with crimp.

Memory is the term used to describe a fiber's ability to "remember" its own form. In other words, it describes whether or not a fiber is able to bounce back from stretching and wear and tear. Wool has great memory and can be used to create stretchy, form-fitting items like hats and socks. A nice hot water bath (be careful not to felt the wool!) will snap wool back to its original form. Fibers like silk and alpaca do not have memory, so they are best for items like shawls and scarves that don't need to stretch or fit snugly. Once silk and alpaca begin to sag or stretch, there's no going back.

1. Cotton

2. Linen

3. Ramie

4. Soy Silk

5. Bamboo Carbon Fiber

6. Nylon (Firestar)

7. Mylar

13

form of fiber preparation. Carded fibers are not as neatly organized as combed fibers. The shorter fibers remain mixed in and, instead of running parallel, the fibers cross over each other. Carding is also referred to as a woolen preparation and produces fuzzier, lighter yarns than combing.

Types of Prepared Fibers

Many fiber preparation names are used interchangeably today, but each has its own definition and characteristics.

Top is a rope of combed fibers. Top is usually fairly dense and about as thick as your wrist.

Roving is a rope of carded fibers. Roving is airier than top, and it's about as thick as a wrist. This is the form of fiber I recommend for beginners. In this form, the fibers are easy to manage and the carded preparation is easy to spin.

Sliver and pencil roving are thin ropes of carded fiber. These preparations are also fairly easy for a beginner, but they

14

are a bit more delicate to handle because they are thinner than regular roving.

Batts are sheets of carded fiber. Most roving, including sliver and pencil roving, started in batt form and were stripped or stretched into thinner pieces. If you buy a batt of fiber, you can separate it into strips for easy spinning.

Raw fibers or loose fibers have not been through any preparation and will need to be processed before they can be used. Raw fiber has not been cleaned and

will generally come in the form of fleeces from sheep and other animals. Loose fiber may have already been cleaned and even dyed, but it still needs to be prepared into a spinnable form. Check the resources on page 125 for places you can learn about processing fiber.

Spinning Tools

Every portion of the spinning process can be done by hand. You can make yarn as long as you have fiber and your own two hands—try it! Pinch off a small piece of fiber. Hold one end between the thumb and pointer finger of your left hand and roll the other end between the thumb and pointer finger of your right hand. *Voilà!* It's yarn! Remember, yarn is simply fiber held together by twist. However, tools make it easier to make more yarn and to make it in a more precise way. Here are a few of my favorite tools. Start with one spindle and then buy or make the rest if and when you need them.

Spindles

Spindles are the original spinning tool, and they are still the tool of choice for many spinners today. While most people can produce yarn faster on a wheel, spindles are much more portable and inexpensive. I recommend starting on a spindle because it is much easier to see and understand the mechanics of spinning. With all their moving parts, spinning wheels distract from the fact that spinning is simply adding twist to fiber to make yarn. Spindles make that process very clear. There are many different types of spindles, and many cultures have their own unique type of spindle. I have highlighted a few of the most common types

of spindle here. Try each before you buy and pick the one that works best for you.

Drop spindles are used to make yarn by spinning suspended from a length of fiber. The spinning spindle twists the fiber, turning it into yarn. If the yarn breaks, the spindle will drop to the ground, so drop spindles need to be somewhat sturdy so they won't break.

Supported spindles are used to make yarn by spinning supported from below. Very thin yarns can be spun on a support spindle because the yarn does not have to support the weight of the spindle. Support spindles are usually spun in shallow bowls or on the spinner's leg.

High-whorl spindles have a whorl located near the top of the spindle. (A high-whorl drop spindle is shown below, at top.) There is very little shaft over the whorl on high-whorl spindles, so most have hooks to secure the yarn because there is not room to make a half-hitch knot (see page 26).

Low-whorl spindles have a whorl located toward the bottom of the shaft. (A low-whorl drop spindle is shown below, at bottom.) Low-whorl spindles seldom have hooks, but they often have a notch in the shaft where the half-hitch knot can be secured.

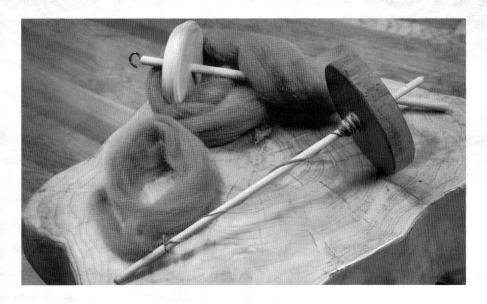

Anatomy of a Spindle

Spindles are extremely simple tools with only a couple different parts. Because of their simplicity, it is easy to make a spindle of your own. Here are the terms you need to know to understand a spindle.

Whorl (1)

The whorl is a weight that helps the spindle to spin longer. Most whorls are round, but they can come in a variety of shapes. Whorls can be made from a variety of materials, but for drop spindles I recommend a break-resistant material. If you'd like to make your own spindle, you can use a CD as a whorl, or try making your own whorl out of wood or polymer clay. To some extent, the weight of the whorl determines what kind of yarn a spindle can make. The weight of a heavy spindle will break very thin yarn, so it is best used with thicker yarns. A light spindle will not spin for very long when you are making a thick yarn and works best when making a thin yarn.

Shaft (2)

The shaft of a spindle goes through the center of the whorl and is used to turn the spindle with a quick twist of the fingers. The shaft also stores the newly spun yarn during spinning.

Hook (optional) (3)

A hook can be added to the end of the spindle's shaft to hold the yarn in place. When yarn is wound onto the shaft, it needs to be secured before spinning can continue. This can be done on spindles without a hook by making a half-hitch knot (see page 26). On a spindle with a hook, the yarn can simply be threaded through the hook.

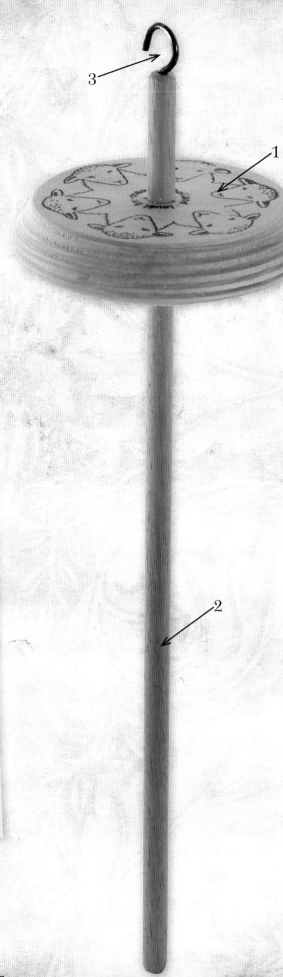

Spinning Wheels

Just as using a spindle is a quicker and more efficient method of spinning than using your hands, spinning wheels are quicker and more efficient than spindles. Spinning wheels take the yarn-making and -managing process to the next level. Instead of a spindle that starts, stops and can even unwind, spinning wheels spin at a constant speed controlled by your feet, leaving both hands free to manipulate the fiber. Spinning wheels also automatically organize the spun yarn, which has to be wrapped by hand on a spindle. Many spinners, myself included, prefer spinning on a spinning wheel for ease and quickness. However, spinning wheels are much more expensive than spindles and aren't as portable. Spinning wheels can also be more difficult for beginners than spindles because of their spinning speed. Once you've learned the basics on a spindle, if you want to do more, more, more! you just may be ready for a spinning wheel. Choosing a wheel is an important (and expensive) decision. Try as many different wheels as you can before buying, and then take home the one that feels best to you.

A Note About Getting Your Wheel Ready to Spin

A spinning wheel, although you may not think of it as such, is a machine. Like most machines, it needs oil to keep working smoothly. On many modern wheels, some or most of the moving parts are sealed and don't need oiling.

I've included some very basic instructions for preparing your wheel for spinning (pages 34 and 35).

As always, it's best to refer to the manufacturer's instructions that came with your wheel for a complete list of parts that will need oil for smooth spinning.

Anatomy of a Spinning Wheel

Each spinning wheel has its own unique look and configuration. There is a short list of parts common to all spinning wheels. The manufacturer of your spinning wheel is the best authority on what parts your wheel has and where you can find them. This is a broad identification list to help you understand your wheel. Take time to get to know your spinning wheel and how to adjust it. If you can't find the answers you need here, contact someone at the store where you bought your wheel or at your wheel's manufacturer.

The **drive wheel** (1) is the biggest moving part of a spinning wheel, and it does just what its name implies—it drives the spinning motion. It is powered by the **treadles** (2), which are connected to the drive wheel by **footmen** (3) and a **crankshaft** (4). Pushing on the treadles (or treadle—some spinning wheels have two treadles, some have one) causes the drive wheel to turn. The turning drive wheel moves the **drive band** (5), which is wrapped around both the drive wheel and the **whorl** (6). On some spinning wheels the tension on the drive band can be adjusted by a **drive band tensioning knob** (7). On others, the tension on the drive band is changed by altering the drive band. The turning whorl moves the **flyer** (8). The size ratio of the drive wheel to the whorl determines how quickly the whorl spins, and therefore how quickly the flyer spins. On traditional wheels, the flyer is supported by **maidens** (9) and the **mother-of-all** (10). On more modern wheels, the flyer may be unsupported at the front end. The flyer is a U-shaped piece that contains a **bobbin** (11), which is where the yarn is stored during spinning. The yarn runs between the spinner's hands and the bobbin through the **orifice** (12) and is then guided to the bobbin through a series of **hooks** (13). Moving the yarn from one hook to another will change where the yarn winds on the bobbin. Some flyers have **eyelets** (14) instead of hooks to guide the yarn. The yarn is wound onto the bobbin when the flyer rotates faster than the bobbin. On Scotch tension wheels, a **brake band** (15) tensions the bobbin, while on a double drive wheel the tension on the bobbin comes from the drive band.

When spinning, it is also handy to have a bottle of oil with a small nozzle on hand for oiling the moving parts, as well as an orifice hook for drawing the yarn through the orifice in the flyer.

Yarn Management Tools

Once your yarn is spun, it needs to be organized for easy storage and use. Yarn can be wound into skeins or balls by hand, but these handy tools make the process faster and easier. If you are a knitter, you may already have some of these items.

A **lazy kate** (1) is used to hold bobbins of singles during the plying process. This keeps the bobbins and singles neat and tidy while the singles unwind from the bobbins. Some lazy kates have a tensioning system for smooth, even unwinding. The advantage to using a lazy kate is that your bobbins won't be rolling all over the floor as you unwind your singles.

A **niddy noddy** (2) is used to wind yarn into a skein. A niddy noddy has three arms: a long central arm and two shorter arms that are perpendicular to each other. The yarn is wrapped around the tips of the two shorter arms to form a loop. This neat organization of yarn is convenient for washing and storing yarn. The advantage of using a niddy noddy is that you get consistently sized skeins and you don't have to listen to someone whine as you wind yarn onto their hands.

A **swift** (3) holds a skein of yarn under tension so it can be wound into a ball. Pulling on the yarn causes the swift to rotate, providing a smooth, even feed of yarn as it is wound. Again, the swift has the no-whine advantage.

A **ball winder** (4) is (not surprisingly) used to wind yarn into a center-pull ball. This convenient machine is quicker than winding a ball of yarn by hand, and many spinners prefer to draw yarn from the center of the ball, an effect that is difficult to achieve through hand winding.

A **wpi gauge** (5) is used to measure the wraps per inch (or wpi) of yarn, a measurement that is to spinning what gauge is to knitting. Usually made of plastic or wood, a wpi gauge is a small rectangle with a 1" (3cm) wide notch. Start with the yarn end at one side of the notch. Wrap the yarn around the gauge, filling the notch from one edge to the other without the yarn overlapping or crowding, but resting in neat, even, vertical lines. The number of wraps that fit in the notch is the yarn's wpi measurement.

Yarn and Fiber Storage

If you aren't going to be using your newly spun yarn or newly purchased fiber right away, carefully consider your storage options. Leaving yarn or fiber out in the open exposes it to minor inconveniences, like dust, and major yarn disasters, like moths and other fiber-devouring insects. Take the same care in storing your yarn as you do in making it, and it will be ready and waiting when you want to create something with it.

Wool wash or gentle soaps (1) and detergents should be used to clean yarn before it is stored. No-rinse washes are quick and convenient, while gentle soaps and detergents are perfect for more heavily soiled yarns. Allow washed yarns to dry completely before storing.

I use **plastic storage bins** (2) to store my fibers and yarns. They are inex-

pensive and widely available in a range of sizes to fit any storage space. I have enough fiber and yarn that I also take advantage of their stackability. Using see-through bins allows you to see what is in each bin without opening it. Snug lids keep out dust and fiber-loving vermin.

Insect-repelling herbs (3) are a great addition to any storage system. Make your own mix, or purchase pre-made pouches full of herbs such as lavender, cloves and mint. Tucking a couple pouches into each storage bin will help keep vermin away. Make sure to also inspect any area where you plan to store fiber and yarn. If you find a moth (or other fiber-eating insect) infestation, rid the area of pests before storing any fiber there.

Spinning Techniques

Spinning is a simple process to understand: Introduce twist into fiber to create yarn. However, understanding spinning with your head and learning to spin with your hands are two completely different animals. I like to compare learning to spin with learning to ride a bike. Understanding how to ride a bike won't get you very far. Yes, you understand that you balance your body over the center of the bike and pedal to make the bike move forward. But you have to teach your body that movement to make it all work. Spinning is the same way—it involves muscle memory. You have to teach your body how to spin, not just your brain. Be patient with yourself and the wool, and keep trying if you have a rough start. One advantage that learning to spin has over learning to ride a bike is that it's pretty hard to fall off a spinning wheel or spindle!

Preparing Fiber for Spindle or Wheel

Before you begin spinning, a little preparation is in order. Preparing your fiber not only gets it ready for the spinning process, but it also gives you valuable information you'll use during spinning. Good prep work makes spinning an easier and more pleasant experience, so don't skip this step!

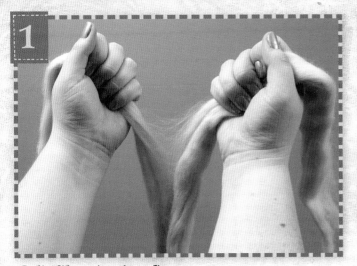

Split fiber (optional)
Many different fiber preparations, such as top, roving and batts, are easier to spin if they are split during preparation. Splitting the fiber mass into thinner strips makes it easier to predraft. However, you do not always want to begin by splitting the fiber. Thinner preparations, such as sliver or pencil roving, do not need to be split, and you may also choose not to split a multicolor top or roving to control the way the colors appear in the finished yarn.

For rope-like preparations like top and roving: Begin by breaking off a 12"–18" (30cm–46cm) length of fiber. Many tops and rovings have natural divisions along the length of the fiber. If you can find one, grasp the fibers on either side and begin to pull the fiber into strips.

If you cannot find a natural division: Start by splitting the top or roving in half lengthwise. Grasp half of the fibers in each hand and start splitting the roving vertically. Move your hands down the length of the fiber every few inches for a neat division.

Find staple length
No matter what fiber or fiber preparation you are working with, the staple length of the fiber is an important piece of information to have while spinning. To find the staple length, grasp a few fibers at the end of your fiber mass and pull them free of the fiber mass. Measure the length of the fibers with a ruler.

Remember this staple length as you are predrafting and drafting. Keep your hands at least as far apart as the staple length plus 2" (5cm). For instance, if the staple length of your fiber is 3½" (9cm), keep your hands at least 5½" (14cm) apart while predrafting and drafting. If your hands are closer together, you may end up pulling on both ends of the fiber, which will just make predrafting and drafting difficult and frustrating because you won't get anywhere, or you'll break the fibers, which will affect the yarn.

Tip

For your first yarns, I recommend splitting the fiber into sections a little thicker than your thumb. Once you get the basics down, you may choose to split fiber into different-sized strips for various reasons, but this is a good starting point.

23

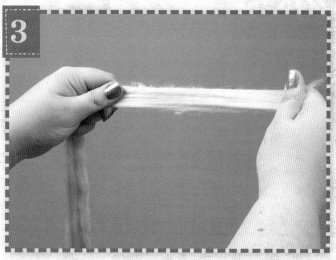

Begin predrafting

To predraft, grasp one end of the strip of fiber with your dominant hand. Place your other hand on the fiber strip at least as far away as the staple length of the fiber plus 2" (5cm). Pull gently on the fibers with your dominant hand. They will begin to glide past one another, thinning the fiber strip. There will be some resistance.

Once you've predrafted the first fibers on the end of the strip, move both hands down the strip approximately 2" (5cm) and predraft those fibers. Continue to move along the length of the fiber, predrafting the entire strip.

Finish predrafting

After a few inches of predrafting, look at your fiber strip. The predrafted portion should be thinner and airier, and you should be able to just see through it. If you see thick spots, go back to those spots and predraft again until the length of fiber is a consistent thickness. Finish predrafting the entire fiber strip.

 Tip

During spinning, you will draft the fibers to thin the fiber mass to the thickness of the yarn you desire. A bit of drafting before spinning, or predrafting, will make the spinning process a bit easier.

During predrafting, there will be some resistance. If you pull too hard, too fast or for too long, you will feel the fibers "give" and pull away from the strip. Try to just thin the fibers without separating the fibers from the strip. It may take a few tries to get just the right amount of tension on the fiber to predraft without separating, so be patient and try, try again. If you're struggling to get the fibers to glide against one another, try separating your hands an extra 1"–2" (3cm–5cm). If that doesn't make predrafting easier, try starting from the other end of the fiber strip. Sometimes it's easier to predraft and draft from one end of the strip than the other.

Spinning with a Spindle

Spinning yarn on a spindle is a great way to learn the spinning process. Spindles are inexpensive, portable and easy to use and understand. Simply start the spindle with a twist of your fingers, and you are spinning! Be patient with yourself, with the spindle and with the fiber as you begin. Remember: Spinning is simple in theory, but it's not just your head that needs to learn to spin—your hands need to learn, too. And also remember that everyone learns differently. If these instructions aren't crystal clear to you, don't give up. Look for spinning videos on the Internet, or seek out a spinner who can teach you in person. I promise, everyone can learn how to spin; it's just a question of finding the right teacher!

Preparing the Spindle for Spinning

All you really need to do to get started with spinning on a spindle is gather together some fiber and a spindle. Some spinners prefer to start spinning without a leader attached to their spindle, and among those who like to use a leader, there is debate about the best type of leader. My preference is to use a leader, and for that leader to be a doubled length of crochet cotton. It is strong, smooth and easy to attach fiber to. It also doesn't add much weight to the spindle. Follow the simple steps below to add a leader to your spindle.

Wrap leader
Cut a piece of crochet cotton approximately 3' (1m) long. Fold it in half and knot the cut ends together. Hold your spindle in front of you and lay the crochet cotton loop over the shaft, with the knotted end close to the shaft. Wrap the crochet cotton loop around the shaft twice.

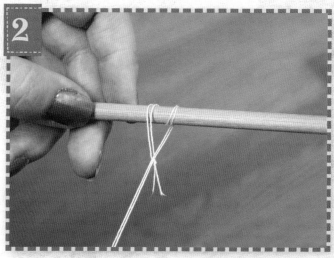

Secure leader
Pull the looped end of the crochet cotton loop through the knotted end of the crochet cotton loop. Snug the crochet cotton to the shaft of the spindle.

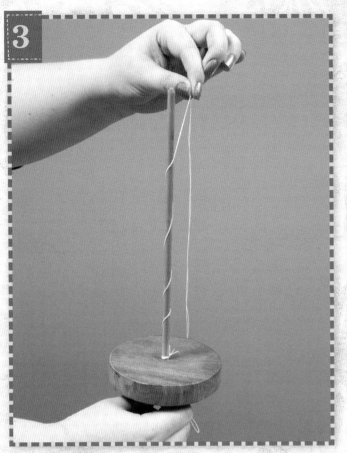

Wrap shaft

Wrap the leader up the shaft of the spindle in a spiral. Wrap the spindle in the same direction you plan to spin (see A Note About Twist Direction below).

Half-hitch knot

Secure the leader around the top of the spindle's shaft with a half-hitch knot. To make the half-hitch knot, loop the leader around your finger, and then turn the loop over so that the portion of the leader wrapped around the spindle crosses over the free portion of the leader. Stick the tip of the spindle's shaft through the loop, and then tighten by pulling on the free portion of the leader.

A Note About Twist Direction

When spinning, you can add twist to the fiber in two different directions.

When you spin your spindle or spinning wheel in a clockwise direction, you are creating Z twist. The twist in the yarn slants in the direction of the center part of the letter Z. When you spin in a counterclockwise direction, you are adding S twist. The twist in the yarn slants in the direction of the center part of the letter S.

To know what direction to spin your yarn, you need to understand the structure of yarn and know what you plan to do with it. First, the structure: Yarn can have many structures—it can be made up of a single strand (called singles yarn), or it can be made up of two or more singles spun together (called plied yarn). The most common way to spin yarn is to spin singles with Z twist, and then to ply with an S twist. This produces yarn that is perfect for knitting. Yarn for crochet is worked in the opposite way, with S-twist singles and Z-twist ply.

Twist direction needs to be alternated. Singles are plied in the direction opposite to which they were spun; Z singles are plied in an S direction; S singles are plied in a Z direction. And if you plan to make a cable yarn, which is two or more plied yarns plied together, then you would alternate direction again in either a Z S Z pattern or an S Z S pattern.

The most important thing to remember is that the final twist influences the final use of the yarn. For example, knitting uses yarn that was spun with S twist as the final twist. So, if you are plying, the ply is the final twist, and it should go in the S-twist (counterclockwise) direction. If you are not plying and plan to knit with singles, you will only be adding twist once, so the first twist is also the final twist. If you plan to knit with singles, they need to be spun with S twist, because knitting requires the final twist to be an S twist.

Starting to Spin

The steps shown below are how I recommend you spin your first few inches of handspun yarn. Normal spinning instructions can be found over the following pages. This is not the normal drop spinning method; this is spinning slowed down so you can see exactly what happens. As you try these few steps, watch the fiber become yarn before your eyes. Spinning yarn on a spindle is much slower and simpler than spinning yarn on a spinning wheel, but it still seems to happen very fast when you are first learning. Slowing down the process for even a few inches will help your spinning education.

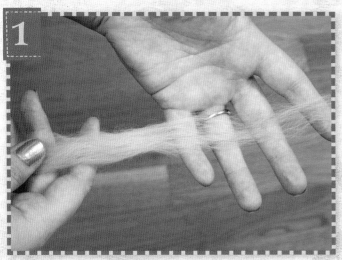

Thin end of fiber
Predraft the first 3"–4" (8cm–10cm) of the fiber strip again until it is half the thickness of the rest of the strip.

Attach fiber to leader
Place the tip of the fiber strip through the looped end of the leader. Fold the thin end of the fiber strip over the leader. Pinch the folded fiber between the thumb and first finger of your dominant hand.

Roll spindle
Sit down in a comfortable chair. Hold the spindle in your nondominant hand and place the shaft of the spindle on your thigh. With the folded end of the fiber pinched, slowly roll the spindle down your thigh. Twist will first begin to enter the leader, and then will transfer to the fiber. When you get close to your knee, pick up the spindle and place it at the top of your thigh. Roll the spindle down your leg again.

Draft fiber
When the fiber between your fingers and the leader is tightly twisted, secure the shaft of the spindle to your leg with your elbow or forearm. Pinch the newly spun yarn with your nondominant hand right where your dominant hand pinches. Use your nondominant hand to hold the twist in that portion of the fiber. Move your dominant hand back along the fiber strip at least as far away from your nondominant hand as the staple length of the fiber plus 2" (5cm) (see page 23). Draft the next few inches of fiber. Pinch the drafted strip of fiber with your dominant hand 2"–3" (5cm–8cm) away from your nondominant hand. Let go of the yarn with your nondominant hand and watch the twist travel towards your dominant hand. These are the basic actions of one method of spinning: Add twist, draft fiber, allow twist to travel to drafted fiber, repeat.

Repeat Steps 3–4 until you are ready to move on.

Drop Spindling Singles

Well, after all of the preparation and practice, you are finally ready to spin! Follow the steps below to spin yarn with a drop spindle. As you begin, be patient and expect some mistakes—they are a natural part of the learning process. Go as slowly as you need to in order to learn this process. And enjoy your first lumpy, bumpy yarns! Many spinners work so hard to perfect their yarn and find out they can't replicate those wonderful first yarns even when they want to.

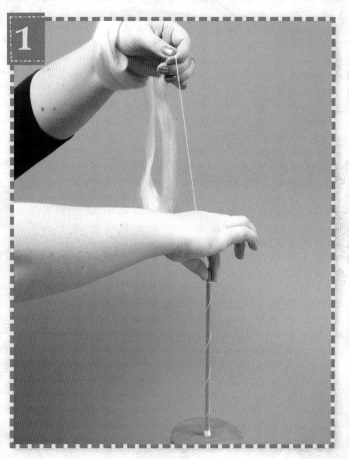

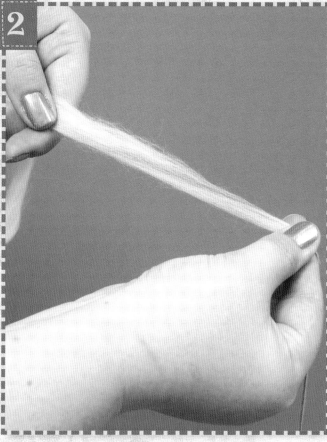

Spin spindle

Before you begin drop spindling, get on your feet—you'll be able to spin a longer length of yarn at one time in this position. Wrap the predrafted fiber tail around the wrist of your nondominant hand, leaving about 12" (30cm) free. Hold the fiber strip in your nondominant hand, and pinch the fiber between your thumb and first finger. With your dominant hand pinch the shaft of the spindle and give it a twist in the direction you want to spin (see A Note About Twist Direction on page 26).

Draft fiber

After getting the spindle started, move your dominant hand back to pinch the fiber directly in front of your nondominant hand. Move your nondominant hand back along the fiber strip at least as far as the staple length of the fiber plus 2" (5cm). Grasp the fiber strip with your nondominant hand, then pull forward with your dominant hand to draft the fiber. Draft the fiber strip down to about twice the thickness you want for your single. For even yarn, draft evenly so that the fiber strip is a consistent width throughout.

Once the fiber is drafted, slide your dominant hand back along the drafted fiber toward your nondominant hand, letting the twist move into the drafted fiber. Move your nondominant hand back again, pull forward with your dominant hand to draft and then slide your dominant hand back to allow twist into the drafted fiber.

Tip

When you are first starting out, it can be difficult to master consistent drafting along with everything else. For now, just concentrate on learning the motions of spinning—you can worry about perfection another time!

Tip

As you move your dominant hand back over the drafted fiber, the amount of pressure you put on the fibers is important. Grasp the fiber firmly enough to keep the twist from moving too quickly into the fibers—don't let the twist travel past your fingers. Also, your fingers should smooth the fibers down a bit before the twist enters them; too much pressure will ruffle the fibers. In her book Spindle Spinning: From Novice to Expert, *Connie Delaney advises holding the "roving in your hand as a live bird," which helped me understand the correct amount of tension to use when I first started spinning.*

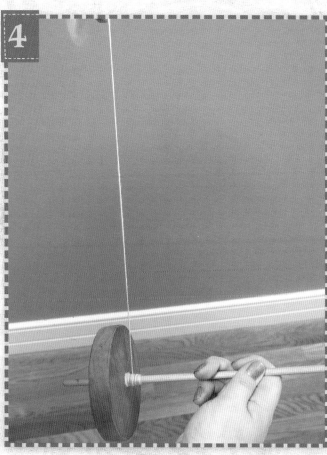

Continue spinning

As you spin, you need to pay attention to a couple of things (as if you didn't already have enough to think about!): the spinning of your spindle and its proximity to the floor. As you spin, keep an eye on your spindle to check that it keeps spinning the direction you started it in. As the spin slows, reach down with your dominant hand and give it another spin.

As you spin, the yarn will get longer and your spindle will, therefore, get closer to the floor. Once your spindle gets within a few inches of the floor, it is time to wind on your yarn.

Wind on yarn

To wind your yarn onto the shaft of the spindle, first stop the spindle from spinning. Grasp the shaft of your spindle in your dominant hand. Sweep the half-hitch knot off the end of the shaft. Rotate the spindle in the same direction you were spinning so that the yarn wraps around the shaft of the spindle, directly against the spindle's whorl. As you spin more yarn, it will form what is known as a "cop," a cone-shaped bundle of yarn. Once you have about 12" (30cm) of yarn left, wrap the yarn up the shaft of the spindle in a spiral, secure the yarn at the end of the shaft with a half-hitch knot and resume spinning. Repeat this process every time the spindle nears the floor.

Tip

Don't let the spindle start spinning in the opposite direction. This will unspin your yarn! If the spindle is spinning too fast, or you need a moment to concentrate on organizing your fiber, feel free to stop the spindle and hold it between your knees or under your arm to keep it from unspinning while you work out whatever problem you may have encountered. Once you are ready to spin again, let the spindle hang from the yarn and start it spinning again.

Joining a New Piece of Fiber

During spinning—when you're a beginner and beyond—it is easy to be a bit overenthusiastic about drafting and pull the fiber strip apart. Even if you don't make that mistake, you will eventually reach the end of your fiber strip, usually before you've made enough yarn to make even the smallest project. This means you need to know how to join a new strip of fiber to the old. Follow these easy steps and you'll be all set. Here, I'm joining on a fiber strip of a different color so that you can easily see how this process works.

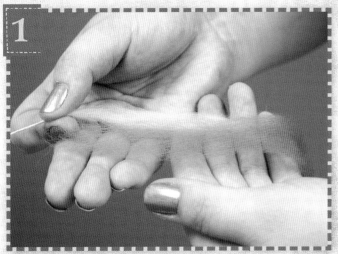

Overlap strips

After predrafting the new strip of fiber, overlap it with the old strip of fiber for several inches. Draft the two strips together to match the width of a single fiber strip.

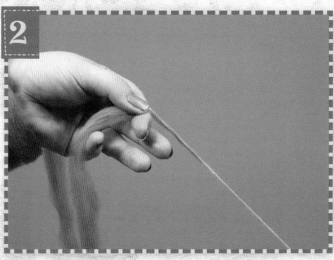

Begin spinning

Begin spinning normally, but as you work, be sure to draft slowly and carefully to ensure that the two strips stay overlapped and draft together.

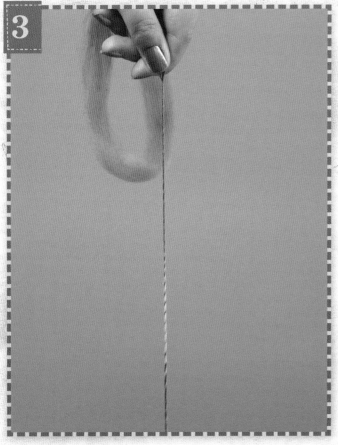

Continue spinning

Once you've spun past the point where the two strips overlap, continue spinning as usual.

Fix or Finish?

FIX: For some solutions to common problems you may encounter while spinning singles, see pages 33 and 40–41. These solutions are shown for wheel-spinning but can be applied to spindle spinning as well. Continue spinning until you have the amount of singles you need for your intended project.

FINISH: If you want to work with the single you've just spun, go to Finishing the Yarn on page 47. If you want to spin a plied yarn, continue with the directions on page 31.

Plying on a Drop Spindle

Once your singles are spun, you can either use those singles, or ply them. I prefer plied yarns for most projects because plying makes yarns stronger. Plied yarns are also easier to balance than singles yarns, which means the yarn is stable, with no extra twist energy. Another advantage of plying is that it is just one more way to work color play into a yarn, and I am always a fan of more color. To show this technique clearly, I use two singles in the following pictures, but you can ply as many singles as you like into a single yarn!

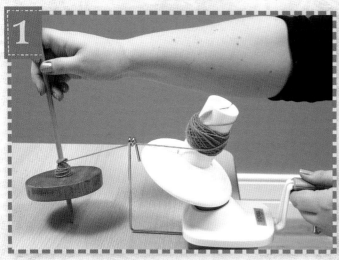

Organize yarn

Before singles can be plied, they need to be organized and controlled in some way. If you have a lazy kate made for spindles, you can use that, but if you're just starting out you can use other methods, as well. You can wind the singles around a cardboard tube, such as an empty toilet paper roll, or onto a storage bobbin. You can also roll the singles into a ball by hand or with a ball winder. Here, I am winding my singles into a ball on a ball winder.

Tension yarn

The second step to organizing the yarn for plying is to contain it. Containing the yarn keeps it from rolling around while you ply. This keeps the yarn clean and close to you so it is easy to control. My favorite no-special-equipment way of containing yarn is using a coffee mug. The yarn can be contained in the mug and tensioned by wrapping the yarn through the handle on its way to the spindle.

Prepare spindle

Once your yarn is ready for plying, you need to get your spindle ready. Follow the steps on page 25, but remember to prepare your spindle to spin in the opposite direction as the one you used to make your singles. Remember, the twist direction needs to alternate from singles to plying (see A Note About Twist Direction on page 26).

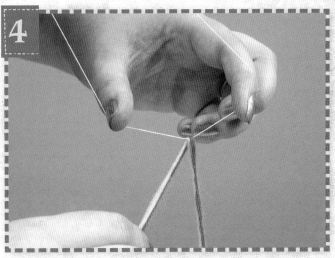

Attach singles to spindle

Pinch the ends of the singles together and place them through the looped end of the leader. Fold the singles over the leader.

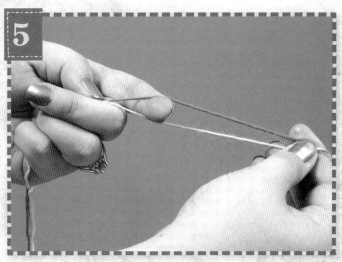

Begin spinning

Pinch the folded singles together with your nondominant hand and start the spindle spinning with your dominant hand. Remember to spin the spindle in the opposite direction used to spin the singles. After getting the spindle started, move your dominant hand back to pinch the singles directly in front of your nondominant hand. Move your nondominant hand back along the singles a few inches. Place your index finger between the singles and grasp the singles with your remaining fingers. It is up to your nondominant hand to keep even tension on the singles so that the ply is balanced. Once the plies are arranged correctly in your nondominant hand, slide your dominant hand back along the singles toward your nondominant hand, letting the twist move into the singles, twisting them together. Once your dominant hand reaches your nondominant hand, pull forward with your dominant hand and then slide your dominant hand back along the singles, allowing the twist into the singles.

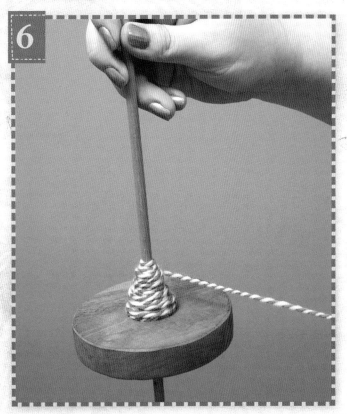

Winding on yarn

When the spindle is nearing the floor, stop the spindle from spinning. Grasp the shaft of the spindle in your dominant hand. Sweep the half-hitch knot off the end of the shaft. Rotate the spindle in the same direction you were spinning so that the plied yarn wraps around the shaft of the spindle, directly against the spindle's whorl, forming a cop as you did with your singles. Once you have about 12" (30cm) of yarn left, wrap the yarn up the shaft of the spindle in a spiral, secure the yarn at the end of the shaft with a half-hitch knot and resume plying.

Fix?

FIX: For some solutions to common plying problems, see pages 44–46. These solutions are shown for wheel spinning, but can be applied to spindle spinning as well.

Managing Fiber While Drop Spindling

While you're drop spindling, it is very easy to get so focused on the motions of spinning that you forget to mind your fiber. And fiber is a wily beast! You have to keep your eye on it all the time or it can turn itself into a terrible snarl. Here's what can happen if your fiber decides to misbehave and how to fix it when it happens.

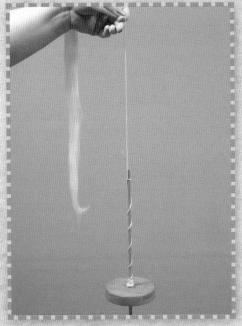

Unminded fiber

This picture shows the setup for disaster: unminded fiber. It's just thrown carelessly over your wrist, tail hanging.

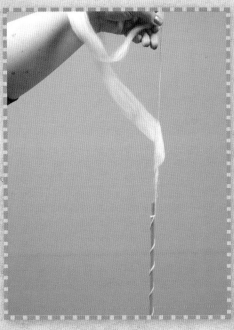

Tangled Fiber

And here's the "disaster:" A slight movement or breeze brings the fiber into close proximity of the spinning yarn and gets sucked into the mix. When this happens, don't panic—it can be easily fixed.

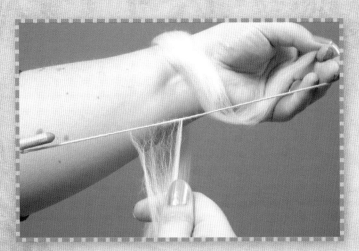

Fix tangled fiber

Stop the spindle. Park the spindle under your arm or between your knees. Keep the spun yarn taut. Grasp the fibers close to the place where they tangle with the yarn. Do not grasp the fibers far away from the yarn—you'll just draft out the fiber stuck in the yarn, and you'll be left with an ugly clump in your yarn. Once you have the fibers in hand, gently pull away from the yarn. The yarn will untwist as you pull, but don't worry; this is a necessary part of the process. It will snap right back to its twisted state when the fibers are separated from it. If any fuzz remains on the strand of yarn, gently pluck it off until the yarn is clean and smooth again. Resume spinning with your fiber carefully organized!

Tip

To keep fiber neat and organized, I recommend keeping it wrapped neatly around your wrist. You can also buy a wrist distaff, which you wear around your wrist like a bracelet. It has a tail that hangs below your wrist that you can wrap the fiber around. It is easier to take on and off than a bracelet of fiber, and it helps keep the fiber neatly organized.

Even if the fiber strip has gotten too short to wrap around your wrist, try to keep it from dangling. If you're wearing long sleeves, you can throw the short tail up over your arm and it will "stick" to your sleeve and not get itself tangled in the mix.

Spinning With a Wheel

Spinning with a spinning wheel makes me feel like a princess in a fairy tale—now. When I first started, it made me feel like banging my head against a wall. I was very glad that I first learned to spin on a spindle, because at least when I sat down at a wheel for the first time, my hands knew what to do (kind of). I recommend starting on a spindle to everyone I know. Once you feel you've learned the basics on a spindle, and if you still want to spin on a wheel, it's time to give it a try. Learning to spin on a spinning wheel is another gradual process—now your whole body needs to learn what to do, not just your hands. Be patient and persistent and you will be rewarded with a wonderful new hobby.

Preparing a Traditional Spinning Wheel

Before you begin spinning on a spinning wheel, you need to prepare it. The best place to find information about preparing your wheel is the wheel manufacturer. They will be able to tell you about everything your wheel needs to stay in proper working order. Here are some of the steps that are common to many traditional wheels.

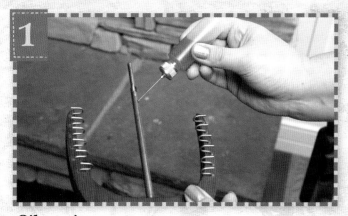

Oil moving parts

One part that needs oiling on every wheel I've encountered is the shaft of the flyer. The bobbin rotates on the shaft of the flyer during spinning. Apply a small amount of oil to the shaft of the flyer. Oil any other unsealed moving parts of the spinning wheel. Your wheel's manufacturer can provide an exact list of what parts need to be oiled, but some common ones are the hinges on the treadle, the areas where the flyer connects to the wheel and where the footmen connect to the crankshaft.

Attach bobbin

Place the bobbin on the flyer. Many bobbins can only be put on the flyer in one direction, so be sure to put the bobbin on correctly. Next, check that the correct whorl is attached to the wheel. On some wheels, like the one pictured here, the whorl screws onto the flyer shaft. On other wheels, the whorl has its own connection to the wheel. Again, refer to the manufacturer's instructions for changing and positioning the whorl.

Begin attaching flyer to wheel

Again, the process of attaching the flyer to the wheel varies from wheel to wheel. Most traditional wheels have two places where the flyer connects to the wheel, one in the front and one in the back. On this wheel, the connection at the back of the flyer is made first. Make the first connection of the flyer to the wheel.

Tip

Each whorl has a different size ratio to the spinning wheel's drive wheel. This ratio determines how quickly the whorl and, therefore, the flyer will rotate. When you're starting out, I recommend using the biggest, slowest whorl you have. You can switch to a faster whorl if you desire as you become more confident with your spinning.

Finish attaching flyer to wheel

Next, make the second connection to attach the flyer to the wheel. For the wheel shown above, this means snapping the orifice end of the flyer into the maiden, which has been oiled.

Check wheel

Before you begin spinning, check that the wheel is set to spin. All moving parts should be properly oiled. The flyer should be perpendicular to the mother-of-all. If necessary, use the drive band tensioning knob to adjust the tension on the drive band. The drive band should be taut but not stretched to its limit. When everything is in its place, you are ready to spin.

Preparing a Modern Spinning Wheel

Modern-style wheels are a bit easier to prepare than traditional-style wheels because they usually have a simpler design. Again, consult the instructions that came with your wheel for exact information on how to prepare your wheel for spinning. If you did not buy a wheel that came new in the box with instructions, check the manufacturer's Web site; you can often download a new set of instructions there.

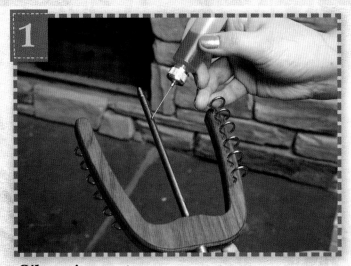

Oil moving parts

As with traditional-style wheels, check the manufacturer's instructions for an exact list of places to oil. Above, I am applying oil to the flyer shaft before attaching the bobbin.

Attach flyer to wheel

Most modern-style wheels have one connection for the flyer. Here, I am screwing the flyer shaft into the shaft that goes through the center of the whorl. Connect the flyer to the wheel securely, following the manufacturer's instructions. Before you begin spinning, check the wheel to make sure that everything is properly attached and oiled.

Practice Treadling

Although you may be eager to get started, there's just one more bit of practice I recommend before you start spinning: practice treadling. Just like your hands learned their job when you learned to drop spindle, this will help teach your feet their job. Soon, keeping the wheel spinning smoothly and in the correct direction will become second nature to you, but in the beginning it can be tricky. You'll be concentrating so much on your hands that suddenly you'll find the wheel spinning in the wrong direction, causing a big mess, because your feet didn't do their job correctly. A little practice beforehand will help with this common spinning blunder.

Start wheel with foot

After a bit of practice, you'll be able to start your wheel in the correct direction with the pressure applied to the treadles, but for now, your wheel may need a kick start to get it going. Sit down in a comfortable chair, preferably one without arms, that is the correct height to work with your wheel. A chair is the correct height if your thighs are parallel to the floor when your feet are resting comfortably, flat on the treadles.

Lift one foot off of the treadle and place it on the outer edge of the drive wheel. Gently move your foot up or down to start the wheel spinning in the direction you desire (see A Note About Twist Direction on page 26). Start treadling with the foot still on the treadles while you move your "kick start" foot back to its treadle. Work the treadles slowly, keeping your feet flat on the treadles. Press down with each foot in turn to push down the treadle and keep the wheel spinning. Practice treadling as slowly as you can without the wheel stopping or reversing direction. Once you feel comfortable treadling in the first direction, practice in the same way with the wheel spinning in the opposite direction.

Start wheel with hand

An alternative to the kick start is to start the wheel with your hand. Place your feet on the treadles, lean forward and gently rotate the wheel in the direction you want to spin. Treadle along with the momentum of the wheel. This method is gentler on your wheel and can also be easier to master because you can start treadling with both feet right away, instead of rushing to get your foot back on a treadle.

Tip

Once you've mastered working in one direction, practice switching directions using only the pressure of your feet. You will not switch directions when you are actually spinning, but if the wheel accidentally switches direction while spinning, learning this action will help you correct that problem quickly. Also practice starting the wheel with just the pressure of your feet, without a kick start.

Spinning Singles on a Spinning Wheel

So your wheel is ready, your fiber is ready (see page 23) and you're ready to begin spinning. Congratulations! Find a comfortable place to set up shop and start getting to know your wheel and wheel spinning. The following steps will help you get started with your first singles. As you start, try to work slowly so that you can see as much of the spinning process as possible. Understanding what is happening as you spin will help you make better yarn.

Tension wheel

Apply tension to the bobbin. On a Scotch drive wheel, this means putting a brake band on the bobbin. On a double drive wheel, this means putting the drive band on the bobbin. In either case, the band on the bobbin should be snug, but not stretched or very taut.

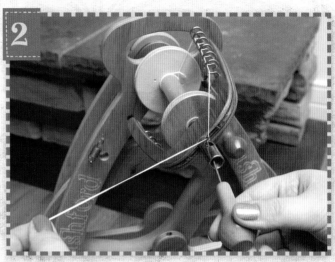

Attach leader

Attach a leader to the bobbin as shown in Steps 1 and 2 on page 25. Push the leader to the back of the bobbin and hook it over the last hook, and then through the remaining hooks on the flyer. Do not wrap the leader around any of the hooks, just through them. If the flyer has an eyelet instead of hooks, move it to the back of the flyer arm and pass the leader through the eyelet. Pull the leader through the orifice, using an orifice hook if necessary.

Attach fiber

Coil your predrafted fiber strip into a nest and place it in your lap. Predraft the first 3"–4" (8cm–10cm) of the fiber strip again until it is half the thickness of the rest of the strip. Place the tip of the fiber strip through the looped end of the leader. Fold the thin end of the fiber strip over the leader. Pinch the folded fiber between the thumb and first finger of your dominant hand. Here, I am pinching the fiber in my left hand. Although I am right-handed and spindle spin like a right-hander, I've always found it more comfortable to spin on a wheel as a left-hander. You can, of course, spin whatever way is most comfortable for you, but most right-handed people do spin with their right hand forward.

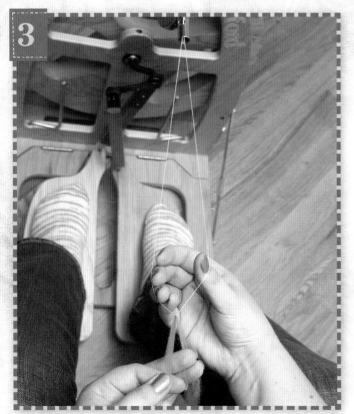

A Note About Tension

The right amount of tension will allow the bobbin to rotate when you are holding the yarn and to hold still when you relax the tension on the yarn to allow it to feed in. It is almost impossible to get just the right amount of tension before you've begun spinning; you need to feel the pull on the yarn to know if it is right. But to start out, aim for a slightly snug tension band, whether it is the brake band or drive band.

Begin spinning

Start the wheel spinning in the direction you desire (see A Note About Twist Direction on page 26). Treadle slowly and evaluate the amount of pull you are feeling from the wheel. If the leader is yanking you toward the bobbin, loosen the tension on the bobbin. If you don't feel any pull, or if the leader is drooping between the wheel and your hands, increase the tension on the bobbin. At this point, you want a steady, persistent pressure that gently pulls on the leader. As you treadle, the twist will first enter the leader and will then enter the fiber folded around the leader. Pinch the fiber with your dominant hand to keep the twist from traveling past your dominant hand.

Begin drafting

Once a bit of twist has entered the fiber folded around the leader, move your nondominant hand behind your dominant hand to grasp the fiber. Keep your nondominant hand at least as far away from your dominant hand as the staple length of the fiber plus 2" (5cm). Pull forward with your dominant hand to draft the fiber and then slide your dominant hand back along the fiber to allow twist into the drafted fiber. This process is exactly the same as spinning singles on a drop spindle (see pages 28–29). The motion you will be performing is: pinch, pull, slide. Continue the motion of pinch, pull, slide to make more yarn. When you reach the end of your fiber strip, or if you accidentally break the fiber strip, join new fiber as shown on page 30.

Check bobbin for yarn

As you pull forward with your dominant hand, the yarn should feed onto the bobbin in the wheel. There should be enough tension on the bobbin that when you move your dominant hand forward, the yarn wraps around the bobbin, storing it. When you move your hand forward, the yarn should not droop or hang down between your hands and the wheel. If the tension isn't high enough to make the yarn feed onto the bobbin, increase the tension on the bobbin. The yarn should wrap neatly around the bobbin next to the first hook the yarn goes through.

Fill bobbin evenly

For best spinning results and tidy yarn storage, move the yarn to a different hook after a nice bump of yarn accumulates at the first hook. Moving the yarn forward on the hooks will make the yarn wrap around the bobbin in a new place, keeping it nicely tensioned and tidy. When you reach the last hook on the flyer, start moving the yarn backward again to fill the bobbin in the opposite direction. Continue like this, moving forward then backward to fill the bobbin, until you've spun all of the yarn you desire, or until the bobbin is full. Do not let the yarn on the bobbin fill beyond the ends of the bobbin. Overfilling a bobbin can at best cause a tangled mess of yarn, and at worst hurt your wheel. Overflowing yarn can wrap around the flyer or flyer shaft. Once a bobbin is full, switch to a new bobbin and start spinning again.

Fix or Finish?

FIX: For some solutions to common problems you may encounter while spinning singles, see pages 40–41. Continue spinning until you have the amount of singles you need for your intended project.

FINISH: If you want to work with the single you've just spun, go to Finishing the Yarn on page 47. If you want to spin a plied yarn, continue with the directions on page 42.

Thinning a Thick Spot in the Yarn

When you're a beginning spinner, lumps and bumps will happen often. And, well, they happen even when you're an experienced spinner. When you're learning to spin, you have so much to concentrate on that paying attention to consistent drafting can be difficult. I advise enjoying the lumps and bumps at first—they're part of being a beginner! But when you've got the motions down, and you want to perfect your technique, I understand wanting to banish the bumps. Here are a few easy steps to smooth yarn.

Stop spinning
When you see a bump appear, stop the spinning wheel. Position the bump between your hands and the wheel.

Untwist fiber
Once twist enters fiber, it becomes yarn, and yarn is stubborn. You need to turn the bump back into roving, top, or whatever it was before it was yarn. Pinch the yarn on either side of the bump. Twist your fingers in opposite directions. The yarn should untwist and puff back up into roving. If the yarn gets more twisted, you're working in the wrong direction. Move your fingers in the opposite direction.

Draft fiber
Once the bump doesn't have any twist in it, gently pull your hands apart slowly to draft the fiber. When the fiber is the width you were spinning the yarn at, stop drafting.

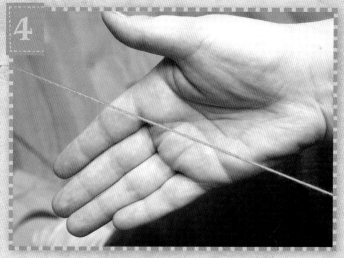

Allow twist into drafted fiber
Let go of the yarn with the hand closest to the wheel, but keep the hand farthest from the wheel pinched around the yarn. Twist stored in the yarn in front of your hand will travel into the untwisted portion. Check the single to make sure the bump is gone and that the width of the single is consistent along the entire length. Continue spinning as normal.

Adding the Right Amount of Twist to Singles

Another detail that can be hard to pay attention to when you first start spinning is the amount of twist in your yarn. After you become comfortable with the motions of spinning, you can concentrate more on adding the right amount of twist. The "right" amount of twist for a yarn depends on what its final use will be. Items that need to stand up to hard wear, like rugs, need to be tightly twisted. More delicate items can be spun with less twist for a softer feel. Also, thinner yarn needs more twist to hold it together.

Fixing amount of twist

After spinning a few feet of yarn, stop the wheel and check the yarn between your hands and the wheel to see how it looks. If the yarn is hard, tightly twisted, or curling and kinking like the yarn shown here, then it is overtwisted. To correct this, you need to release some of the twist.

Without spinning the wheel, draft out some fiber, and then move your dominant hand back along the drafted fiber, letting the excess twist run into the drafted fiber. Continue to do this until the yarn has the proper amount of twist. To prevent this in the future, you can increase the tension on your bobbin so that the yarn is fed onto the bobbin before it acquires too much twist, you can switch to a larger whorl so less twist is added per treadle, or you can treadle slower.

If your yarn is drifting apart or looks like roving with a tiny amount of twist, you are not getting enough twist in the yarn. To add more twist to the yarn, treadle the wheel without letting the yarn feed onto the bobbin until it has the proper amount of twist. To prevent this in the future, you can decrease the tension on your bobbin so that the yarn doesn't feed onto the bobbin before it has enough twist, you can switch to a smaller whorl so that more twist is added per treadle, or you can treadle faster.

Fixing a Wrapped Hook

When you are spinning on a wheel, if the yarn stops feeding onto the bobbin, the two main causes are improper tension on the bobbin or a wrapped hook on the flyer. It is very common for yarn to wrap around a hook on the flyer when the wheel is stopped and started. Fortunately, this problem is very easy to fix. Follow these easy steps to get right back to spinning.

Check hooks

If your yarn has stopped feeding onto the bobbin, stop the spinning wheel. Check the path of the yarn through the flyer. The yarn should travel through the hooks to the orifice, not around any hooks as shown above.

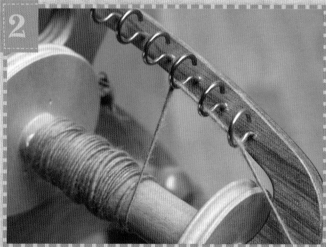

Correct yarn path

Unwrap the yarn from the hook it is caught on and adjust it so it runs through the hooks correctly, as shown above. Restart the spinning wheel. If the yarn still won't wind onto the bobbin, check the drive band and brake band to make sure they are in their proper places and have the correct amount of tension.

Plying on a Spinning Wheel

Singles spun on a wheel gain the same benefits from plying as singles spun on a spindle. Plying strengthens yarn, helps to balance twist and also adds a new level of color play. As with plying on a spindle, you can ply together as many singles as you like. Here, I am using two singles of different colors so you can easily see how plying works.

Create plied sample

Just as with singles, the "right" amount of twist to ply with depends on the final use of the yarn. However, you can get a good idea of how much twist to use on your first practice yarns by making a plied sample with your singles. To make a plied sample, unwind some of the freshly spun singles from the bobbin. Loop the yarn around your finger and bring the single back alongside itself.

Review plied sample

Remove your finger from the single and let it wind around itself. Cut the sample from the remaining singles and save it. The singles had a certain amount of twist energy stored in them; when you released that energy, the singles plied together until the energy in the singles was balanced by the ply energy. If you use approximately the same amount of twist to ply the remaining singles, your yarn should be balanced. As you ply, compare the yarn on the wheel to this sample.

Prepare singles

Before you begin plying, you need to organize the singles. A lazy kate is a very helpful tool that holds bobbins with singles during plying. All lazy kates hold the bobbins in place while allowing them to rotate freely as the singles are drawn off. Some kates also have a tension system to control the rate at which the bobbin spins. Here, I have placed the singles on the built-in lazy kate on my spinning wheel.

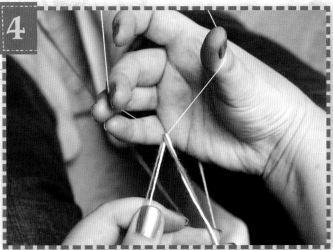

Attach singles

Once your singles are organized, draw the singles off the bobbin just far enough to reach the orifice. Pinch the ends of the singles and thread them through the looped end of the leader. Fold the singles over the leader.

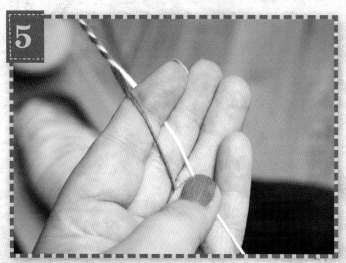

Begin plying

Pinch the folded singles together with your dominant hand and start the wheel spinning. Remember to spin the wheel in the direction opposite of that used to spin the singles. Place your nondominant hand on the singles a few inches behind your dominant hand. After enough twist has entered the folded singles to secure them to the wheel, slide your dominant hand back and position your hand and the singles properly. (You may need to stop the wheel to give yourself time to do this.) Place the index finger of your dominant hand between the singles and pinch the singles between your remaining fingers and thumb. Use both hands to keep even tension on the singles so that the ply is balanced.

Once the plies are arranged correctly in your dominant hand, start spinning again. As twist builds up in the yarn, slide your dominant hand back along the singles toward your nondominant hand, letting the twist move into the singles, twisting them together. Once your dominant hand reaches your nondominant hand, pull forward with your dominant hand, allowing the plied singles to feed onto the bobbin, and then slide your dominant hand back along the singles, allowing the twist into the singles.

Continue plying

Continue to ply using the pinch, pull, slide hand motions until you reach the end of your singles. Keep an eye on the plied yarn to make sure the same amount of twist is being used to ply the yarn as you see in your plied sample. For greater control over the singles, you can also pinch them between your index finger and thumb while plying. Be careful to keep even tension on each single.

43

Fixing a Kink During Plying

There are many common problems you may encounter while plying. One is a kink in a single ply of the yarn. This occurs when one of the singles doesn't have enough tension on it and folds over itself, just like when you make a plied sample. Once the yarn is finished, these kinks can be difficult to fix, but if you catch one while you are plying, it is easy to make your yarn as good as new.

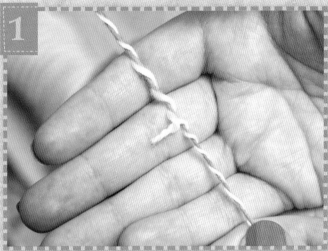

Find the error
When you see an error of this type, bring the wheel to a stop with the flawed portion of yarn between the wheel and your hands.

Unwind ply twist
Take a single ply of the yarn in each hand and pull the plies apart. This will back the twist up toward the wheel and the error. Continue to pull the plies apart until you reach the error. Put tension on the kinked ply until it straightens out.

Continue plying
Reposition the singles in your hand for plying and resume plying, keeping even tension on both singles.

Adding the Right Amount of Twist to Plied Yarn

The amount of twist entering the plied yarn is an easy detail to overlook when you are mastering this new skill. Once you are comfortable with the motions and you are ready to focus on perfecting your yarn, amount of twist is one of the first things you should turn your attention to. The amount of ply twist not only influences how the yarn looks, but it also affects how the yarn feels and how much wear and tear it will stand up to.

Balanced yarn

A balanced yarn has the perfect balance between singles twist and ply twist. The two different directions of twist exert the same amount of energy, causing the energies to balance each other. Balanced yarn will not curl back on itself when it is not under tension. To test your plied yarn to see if it is balanced, stop the spinning wheel and move your hands closer to the orifice so the yarn can hang down. If it hangs down in a U shape without twisting, it is balanced.

Fixing undertwisted yarn

The yarn in this example is undertwisted. The plies only wrap loosely around each other, and when this yarn is used it will be easy to separate the plies, weakening the yarn. Although a softly plied yarn does have its uses, this example is far too underplied. If your yarn looks like this, it can be corrected by adding more ply twist.

To fix underplied yarn, treadle the wheel without letting the yarn feed onto the bobbin until it has the proper amount of twist. To prevent this in the future, you can decrease the tension on your bobbin so the yarn doesn't feed onto the bobbin before it has enough twist, you can switch to a smaller whorl so more twist is added per treadle, or you can treadle faster.

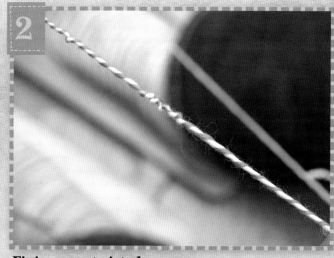

Fixing overtwisted yarn

The yarn in this example is overtwisted. It has so much twist that it is corkscrewing on itself. Tightly plied yarns can have their benefits, such as long wear, but even purposely overtwisted yarn should not corkscrew back on itself. To correct this, you need to release some of the twist.

Without spinning the wheel, move your dominant hand back to allow the twist to run into unplied singles. Continue to do this until the yarn has the proper amount of twist. To prevent this in the future, you can increase the tension on your bobbin so the yarn is fed onto the bobbin before it acquires too much twist, you can switch to a larger whorl so less twist is added per treadle, or you can treadle slower.

Plying with Even Tension

Another detail that can be hard to master during your first plying attempts is keeping even tension on each ply. Singles plied with even tension coil around each other, forming a fairly smooth yarn. Although your first yarns may be lumpy and bumpy, even tension will help smooth some of that out. Uneven tension on singles during plying will result in lumpy yarn, with one ply going straight and the other wrapped around it in loops.

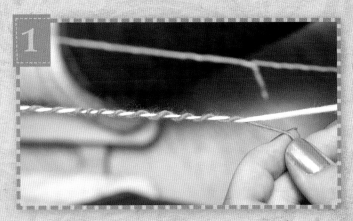

Correct tension

If you notice one single coiling around another instead of both singles coiling around each other, stop the spinning wheel. If just a short section has been badly tensioned, you can pull the two plies apart until you are past the uneven section, and then carefully ply them again under even tension. If a large section of the plied yarn has uneven tension, correct the tension issue and continue plying, leaving the unevenly plied section as is. Unplying a large amount of yarn is difficult and likely to result in a bigger disaster than uneven plying. To correct a tension issue, try repositioning the singles in your dominant hand as shown in either Step 5 or Step 6 on page 43. Resume spinning, using both hands to keep tension on the singles.

Skeining Yarn

After a yarn is spun, it needs to be finished. Before finishing, however, the yarn needs to be organized, or you'll end up with a big, knotted mess. Skeining yarn is an easy way to organize it. I prefer to wind a skein on a niddy noddy; it makes consistently sized skeins, it is portable and it is easy to use. You don't need special equipment, however. You can wind a skein around the back of a chair, or around the hands of a very patient significant other or friend.

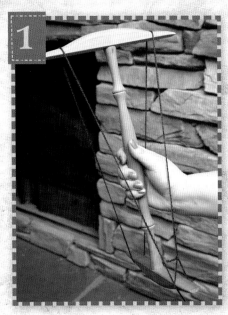

Begin skein

Tie a loop in the end of the yarn. Put the loop over one arm of the niddy noddy. Hold the niddy noddy around the center post with one hand and wind the yarn around the arms of the niddy noddy. Work in a single direction, moving the yarn up and down over the arms without crossing the strands of yarn.

Finish skein

When you reach the end of the yarn you've spun, tie the two ends of the yarn together to secure the skein. To complete preparations for yarn finishing, tie the skein with at least 4 figure-eight ties as shown on page 57.

Finishing the Yarn

After spinning, yarn needs to be finished to set the twist and prepare it for whatever its next incarnation will be, whether it will be woven, knitted, etc. Finishing involves washing, drying and, if you're not using the yarn right away, preparation for storage.

Wash and dry yarn

Once the yarn is skeined, wash it in a basin with warm water and a gentle cleanser; put the yarn into the filled basin, and do not run water over it. Wash the yarn once with soap (you can wash it with soap more than once if it is heavily soiled) and then rinse the yarn until all of the soap is removed. After the yarn is clean, squeeze out as much excess water with your hands as you can without wringing or twisting the yarn. Wrap the yarn in a dry towel to press more water out of it. Hang the yarn and weight the skein. Do not use a heavy object that will stretch the yarn; use something just heavy enough to straighten the yarn.

Prepare yarn for storage

Allow the yarn to dry completely. Many natural fibers, including wool and silk, can feel dry before they are, so let the yarn hang for at least 24 hours. If you are in an especially cold or humid environment, which will cause the yarn to dry slowly, allow more than 24 hours for the yarn to dry. Once the yarn is completely dry it is ready to use. If you are not going to be using the yarn right away, I suggest coiling the skein for neat and tidy storage. To coil the skein, place a hand at each end of the skein and start twisting the ends of the skein in opposite directions.

Store yarn

To finish coiling a skein, fold the twisted skein in half, pull one end through the other and let the skein coil back on itself. This produces a neat bundle of yarn for storage. Although you may be tempted to leave your handspun out so you can admire it, I suggest storing it in a sealed container to protect it from dust, dirt and fiber-eating pests. Fiber-eating pests are very common, especially in older homes, and it's heartbreaking to find a skein of yarn that a pest has nibbled on—ask me how I know! For storage suggestions, see page 21.

A Note About Washing Yarns

Most animal fibers can be felted, so be very careful not to introduce agitation or temperature changes during the wash. I prefer to use dish soap or Woolite to wash my handspun yarns, but there are many specialized products for washing yarns, including no-rinse washes. While washing, try not to produce too many suds; they are hard to rinse out of yarn.

DYE

Dyeing reminds different people of different things. For some, it feels like science or chemistry. Others see it as a chance to act out a childhood dream of becoming a mad scientist. For still others, dyeing is like alchemy: a mix of science and magic. And for many it is art, whether that art is the act of dyeing itself or using dye to create an artist's palette in wool (or silk, or cashmere…). For me, dyeing is all of these things.

Unfortunately, dyeing is also intimidating to some people. I want to take that fear away, because dyeing is a fun and easy way to take creative control over your fiber projects. Whether your concern is safety, space or money, there are solutions that can make dyeing accessible to you. There are safe, nontoxic dye alternatives that are great for homes with kids or critters. I'll show you dyeing methods that can be squeezed into even the tiniest apartment kitchen. And there are many inexpensive dyes worth their weight in gold. The tools and equipment you need to start dyeing are as close as your local kitchen goods store. If you have the will to dye, there's a way. As an added bonus, all of these materials and methods can be used on fiber, handspun yarn or commercial yarn, so you can put your special stamp on a project anywhere in the process.

Once you dive into dyeing, you'll never again be limited by the colors available in your local yarn store. You can create a veritable rainbow of fiber and yarn for your crafting pleasure. Try dyeing and you'll add another level of creativity, customization and fun to your crafts.

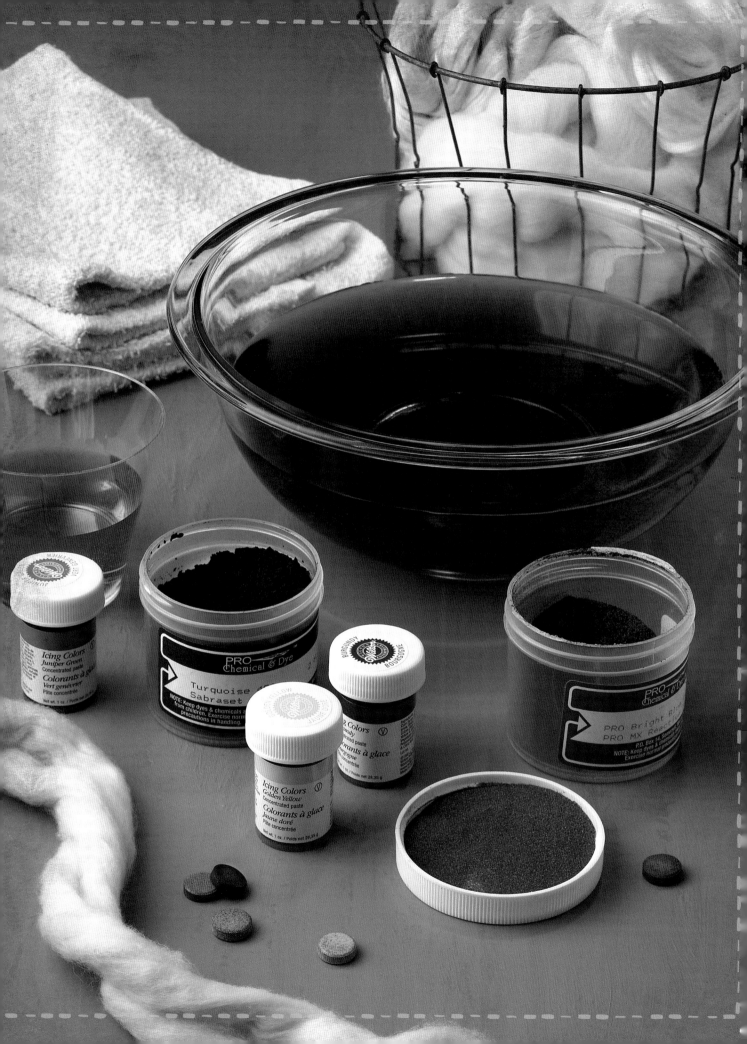

Dyeing Materials and Tools

Dyeing can be a very simple process. If you've ever spilled red wine or grape juice on your favorite sweater, you know just how easy it is! At the most basic level, you need a dye, a material to dye, a container to hold them together, and something to convince the two to stay together, such as heat. There are, of course, many variations for each of those ingredients. Here is some basic information about the things you should have on hand to embark on a successful dyeing adventure.

Dyeing Materials

Crafters who take up dyeing have a wide variety of materials to choose from today. This was not always the case, and dyers today are lucky to have so many options. However, it can be difficult to narrow down all of those choices to find exactly the right material to fulfill your dyeing needs. Take into account what you want to dye, where you will be doing your dyeing and how often you plan to dye to narrow down the options to the one that is right for you.

Dye is any substance that can be used to permanently impart color to another substance. As this broad definition implies, there are many substances that can be used to dye fiber and yarn. The first and most important distinction is whether the dye is made for plant (cellulose-based) fibers or animal (protein-based) fibers. Some dyes can dye both types of fiber, but the proper dye auxiliary chemicals must be used. Choose the correct dye or auxiliary for your fiber and you are off to a great start. For chemical dyes, the dye packaging should indicate what type of fiber the dye is for. For dyestuff like food-safe dyes, which are not labeled for dyeing fiber, try experimenting, or check the Internet to find the results of the experiments of other intrepid dyers. Usually, you will get some color if you use dye on a fiber it is not meant for, but it will not be as bold a color as you would get using the proper dye for the fiber.

In addition to dye and auxiliary, you also need some simple H_2O. Water is used to turn dye into a dye bath. In most cases, normal tap water is just fine for dyeing. However, if you have very hard or very soft water, or if you want precise, predictable results, distilled water is the best choice.

Natural Dyes

If you prefer to go all natural, there are many substances from nature that can be used for dyeing. Plant materials such as indigo and turmeric can be used to impart color to fiber. Used alone, most natural substances do not provide a very deep or rich color. Adding chemical auxiliaries will provide deeper colors. Most natural dyes can be used to dye both cellulose- or protein-based fibers, as long as the proper auxiliary is added. Natural dyes can be unpredictable because the amount of color imparted will vary based on where the material was grown, how old it is and what kind of growing season the plant had. See Resources on page 125 for sources of further information on natural dyes.

Alternative Dyes

Many crafters are concerned about the safety of dyes and chemical auxiliaries, especially if they are dyeing in a space shared with children or pets. Using food-safe dyes can alleviate many of those concerns. Products such as Wilton Icing Colors, Kool-Aid or Easter egg dye tablets and auxiliaries like vinegar are safe for food prep surfaces and won't leave behind any harmful chemicals. However, the variety of colors available in some of these products is limited, and getting an intense color can take a large amount of dye. Food-safe dyes are best for protein-based fibers like wool and silk.

Chemical Dyes

Chemical dyes are the best choice for consistent results, but they may not be the best choice for some dyers. There are safety concerns with some chemical dyes, and they cannot be used with any equipment that will be used for food preparation. They can also be complicated to use, with different auxiliaries to add for best results. Some chemical dyes are also more expensive than other types of dyes. However, for dyers who dye large quantities of fiber or yarn and want consistent, predictable results, chemical dyes are wonderful. Chemical dyes are made for use with either cellulose- or protein-based fibers.

There are inexpensive, all-in-one chemical dyes available today, and I think these are the best choice for a beginner. The auxiliaries are mixed in with the dye, so you only need to add water, and you don't need to store a bunch of separate components between dye sessions. There are many colors available, so you can choose to either buy several individual colors, or buy a few colors and mix your own dye palette. For the dyeing techniques in this book, I used Country Classics dyes, a simple-to-use, all-in-one dye that has yielded great results for me.

Blue dye on white, gray and pink top

Adventures in Dyeing

Fiber and yarn are both great candidates for the dyepot. You can dye fiber before spinning it, yarn after spinning it, or commercial yarn. As long as the fiber or yarn is composed of cellulose- or protein-based fibers, you can dye it. Because dyes are only good for one or the other, a fiber or yarn blend that includes both cellulose- and protein-based fibers will dye unevenly, so keep that in mind when selecting a victim for the dyepot. If you're looking for unique results, it can be fun to experiment with these plant/animal blends, but if you want predictable results, these blends aren't for you. When dyeing, you'll get the clearest, most vibrant colors by dyeing white or cream fiber or yarn.

Don't limit yourself to just white, though. Overdyeing a colored yarn or fiber can yield interesting and beautiful results. Dyeing light gray or brown fibers creates rich, muted colors. Overdyeing pastels can produce interesting color play. Don't be afraid to experiment and have fun.

Dyeing Tools

You only need a few tools to dye successfully, but don't be surprised if you find yourself acquiring quite a few tools. Natural-born experimenters won't be able to resist trying new, ingenious ways to dye fiber and yarn. Here are a few tools to get you started, but be prepared to find yourself eyeing cooking tools in a whole new way once you start dyeing.

Heat Sources

Many dyes need some encouragement to introduce themselves to fiber. For some dyes and fibers, time will simply be enough; if you leave fiber soaking in dye long enough, they're bound to stick together. Chemicals can also force dye and fiber to commingle. For most home dyers, heat is the easiest, most reliable way to join dye and fiber. These common heat sources can help you in your dye journeys.

A stove or hot plate can be used to heat a dye bath quite successfully. This method is slower than heating dye in the microwave, but it is also more controllable and predictable. Also, a stovetop can be used for cooking after the dyeing is done, making it the only heat source that stays food-safe after dyeing.

A microwave is a quick, convenient heat source for dyeing. A microwave also

takes up much less room than a stove if you are setting up a studio for dyeing somewhere other than a kitchen. Many dyers warn against using a microwave for food once it has been used for dyes. Dye particles can deposit on the walls and ceiling of the microwave during dyeing and then redeposit on food later. Metal tools and containers cannot be used for dyeing in a microwave.

A crockpot is just as convenient for dyeing as it is for cooking. Pop in some fiber and dye, turn it on and let it work its magic. Crockpot dyeing does not require the careful monitoring of stovetop and microwave dyeing, but it does take longer than the other methods. Like a microwave, a crockpot that has been used for dyeing should not be used for food.

Vessels

Once you've selected a dye, a fiber and a heat source, you need to pick a vessel in which to bring all of those things together. A vessel needs to have plenty of room to hold both the dye and the fiber or yarn, plus some room for the water to rise when it begins to boil. A vessel also needs to be heatproof to stand up to the heat applied to the dye bath. Choose inexpensive items for dye vessels, because they cannot be used for food purposes once they've been used for dyeing.

Pots are used for stovetop dyeing. Choose pots made from nonreactive materials like stainless steel. A pot used for dyeing should be sturdy with strong handles and a tight-fitting lid.

Bowls and dishes made from heat-safe glass such as Pyrex are perfect for microwave dyeing. For dyeing fiber or yarn a solid color, a heat-safe glass mixing bowl works well, while shallow casserole dishes work well for sprinkle dyeing and hand-painted yarn and fiber.

Plastic wrap is used to contain hand-painted fiber and yarn while it is heated to set the dye. The plastic wrap holds in steam to evenly heat the yarn or fiber and also keeps the different dye colors separate for clear colors in the finished product.

A steamer basket or insert can be used to hold yarn or fiber inside another vessel to keep it out of boiling water and expose it to steam to set the dye. A steamer basket with a handle is convenient for easy removal. The basket should be made from a nonreactive material like stainless steel.

A sink or washbasin will be needed after dyeing is complete to rinse the dyed yarn or fiber. The sink or washbasin should be made of a nonporous material to prevent any excess dye from staining its surfaces.

Other Tools

Just a few more items, and you'll be ready to dye! These items aren't necessary, but they will make dyeing easier and will help you get more predictable, repeatable results, which is important when you create the Perfect Color and want to be able to do it again.

Soap can be used to help prepare fiber and yarn for dyeing. Soap opens fiber up to accept the dye more easily and evenly. Special products for dyeing are available, such as Synthrapol, but I have had great results using good ol' dishwashing liquid.

A thermometer will help you monitor the temperature of a dye bath so you stay within optimal temperature range while dyeing. I recommend a quick-read digital thermometer for ease of use. It's a real pain to let all the heat out of a pot in the form of steam while you wait for a thermometer to reach the correct reading.

Measuring tools like teaspoons, tablespoons and measuring cups are useful for measuring the amount of dye and water for a dye bath. If you are a free-spirited dyer, you can certainly eyeball your quantities, but for predictable, repeatable results, measuring is the best bet.

A scale is a useful tool for measuring the amount of fiber or yarn to be dyed. The proportion of fiber to dye is important when determining depth of shade, so for repeatable results, knowing that proportion is invaluable. I recommend a scale that weighs in grams for accuracy.

Disposable cups and spoons are quick, easy tools to use when mixing dyes. Because you can throw them away after use, you don't have to worry about cross-contaminating your next set of dyes.

Dyeing Techniques

If you've been intimidated in the past by dyeing, fear no more! In the following pages, I provide a road map to guide you on your dyeing journey. Follow these easy steps and you're sure to have great dyeing results with some fun along the way. To be able to repeat your favorite results, take notes throughout the process so you'll know just how to get the same great colors over and over again.

Preparing Fibers for Dyeing

Dyeing, like many things, is much easier with a little preparation. Following these steps will result in even dyeing. However, also like many things, these instructions come with a "but" attached. Prepare your fibers and yarns for even dyeing results, BUT if you don't want even dyeing results, don't prepare your fibers and yarns. Presoaking opens up fibers to accept dyes evenly. If you want a semisolid, mottled look to your fiber or yarn (and that look is quite popular), throw it straight into the dye pot as is. The only hard and fast rule to preparing to dye is that yarn must be skeined before dyeing otherwise you'll end up with a tangled mess.

Skein yarn

Wind the yarn to be dyed around a niddy noddy to form a skein (see Skeining Yarn on page 46). Loosely tie thick string or twine around the skein in at least four places—more ties equals less tangling. To further prevent yarn tangles, you can crisscross the ties through the yarn. Use a square knot to secure the ties.

Bundle fiber

Bundle the fiber to be soaked before dyeing by forming a figure eight with the fiber. Wrap the tail of the fiber around the middle of the bundle, and tuck the end into the wraps to secure it.

Soak yarn or fiber

Fill a tub with warm (but not hot) water. When you have the desired amount of water, shut off the water and add the soap or Synthrapol (you want to avoid forming suds). Following the manufacturer's instructions, add any other additives or auxiliaries required for the dye you will be using. Soak the yarn or fiber in the water. For most plant and animal fibers, 30 minutes will be enough to completely saturate the fibers. Soak silk and other slippery fibers for at least 8 hours for best results.

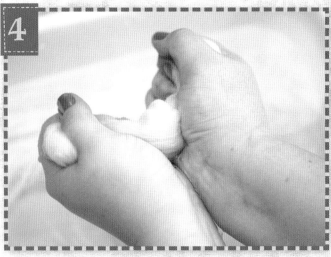

Press out excess water

When the soak is complete, squeeze as much excess water out of the fiber or yarn as you can. Do not wring or agitate the fiber or yarn too much or felting may occur.

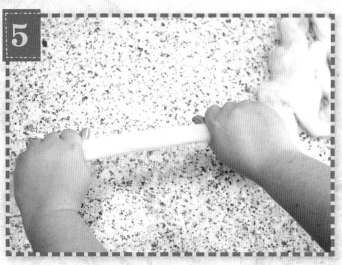

Straighten fiber or yarn

Smooth yarn for dyeing with quick snap of the skein to neaten it up. Roving will grow a bit lumpy and mangy looking during its soak. A series of gentle tugs along the length of the roving will straighten it out. Be very careful not to pull the roving apart as you straighten it.

Depth of Shade Chart

When buying dye, it is often hard to know what you are getting. Dye powders seldom resemble the finished dyed product. Because of this, most dye companies have color cards available for their dyes. These cards have samples of yarns dyed with each color of dye available. These cards are a great starting place to see what you can do with a particular dye, but they don't tell the whole story. Color cards usually only show one sample for each dye, and that sample is usually on the dark end of the spectrum of shades available with that dye. The chart below shows the different depths of shade possible with one color of dye (Country Classics Spring Green).

| 1 oz. (28g) white fiber dyed with **1 teaspoon of dye** | 1 oz. (28g) white fiber dyed with **¾ teaspoon of dye** | 1 oz. (28g) white fiber dyed with **½ teaspoon of dye** | 1 oz. (28g) white fiber dyed with **¼ teaspoon of dye** |

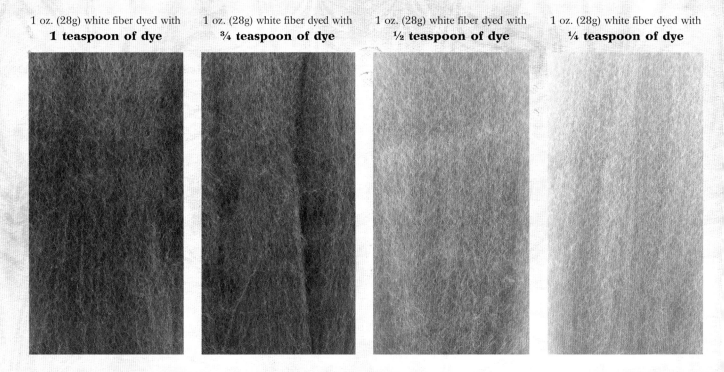

Guidelines for Dyeing Single Colors by Stovetop, Microwave and Crockpot

While dyeing a single color by any of the methods provided in this book, you should follow these guidelines:

Dyes: All dyes should be dissolved in very hot water. Some dyes can be very difficult to dissolve, so be patient. If all of the powder is not dissolved, your results can be splotchy and uneven. For particularly difficult dyes, place them in a container with a tight-fitting lid and shake them instead of stirring them.

Placing yarn: Do not cram or crumple the fiber or yarn, or you may get uneven dyeing results.

Adding water: The amount of water you add will not influence the depth of shade in this type of dyeing—the dye-to-fiber proportion will determine the depth of shade. However, the fibers should be covered completely by the water. Neatly arrange the fiber or yarn in the vessel for even dyeing results. If the dye bath does not completely cover the yarn or fiber, push the yarn or fiber to the side of the pot and add more water to the side without fiber or yarn. Do not pour water or dye directly on the fiber or it may felt.

Heating the dye: Many dye manufacturers, including the makers of Country Classic Dyes, indicate that the dye bath should be brought to a boil. I prefer not to boil dye baths. The agitation from the boiling water can cause delicate fibers to felt. Instead, I heat the dye bath to 180–190 degrees Fahrenheit (82-88°C). The dye process can take longer at this temperature, but I think the difference in the finished product is worth the extra time. Sample to find out which method you prefer.

Checking the dye bath: Pulling a sample of the dye bath out in a white spoon is the easiest way to check the water for dye. If the water has color in it, continue to heat the dye bath. If the yarn or fiber rises partially out of the dye bath when you check it, gently push it back down into the dye bath with the white spoon.

Exhausting the dye bath: When the water in the pot is clear, the dye bath has exhausted, which means all of the dye has been absorbed by the yarn or fiber. This is the optimal situation in dyeing because it means that you are not wasting any dye and you know exactly how much dye is in the fiber, meaning you can replicate the results. For information on why a dye bath may not exhaust and how to handle those situations, see page 71.

Dyeing a Single Color on the Stovetop

Dyeing on the stovetop is a great place to begin your dyeing education. Stovetop dyeing is a slow method that is easy to control and observe, so you'll be able to stay on top of things easily. Plus, you don't need to invest in a lot of equipment to get started. All you need are disposable cups and spoons for mixing dye, measuring spoons for measuring dye and a nonreactive pot for heating the dye bath.

Prepare to dye
Prepare the yarn or fiber for dyeing if desired (see pages 57–58). Measure out the dye powder and place it in a disposable cup. Dissolve the dye powder in very hot water.

Combine dye and fiber or yarn
Pour the dissolved dye into the pot. Add enough water to the pot to cover the fiber, with some extra for steam loss. The amount of water you add will not influence the depth of shade in this type of dyeing—the important proportion here is the dye-to-fiber proportion. Place the fiber or yarn in the pot. Neatly arrange the fiber or yarn.

Heat dye bath
Slowly heat the dye bath to 180–190 degrees Fahrenheit (82–88°C). Once the dye bath has reached the proper temperature, hold the dye bath at that temperature and regularly check the water with a white spoon to see if all of the dye has been absorbed. Keep a lid on the pot whenever you are not checking on the process.

Finish dyeing
When the water in the pot is clear, the dye bath has exhausted. Turn off the heat source, cover the pot and allow the dye bath to cool to room temperature. Rinse and dry the dyed fiber or yarn (see page 70).

Tip

Remember, once something has been used for dyeing, it should not be used for cooking. Pots, measuring spoons, etc., should be clearly marked "dyeing only" once they have touched dye.

Dyeing a Single Color in the Microwave

The microwave is my preferred heat source when dyeing yarn or fiber a single color. It is the quickest method and if you use small vessels, such as glass jars, you can run several dye baths at once. Pyrex mixing bowls also work well for dyeing a single color in the microwave. Temperature changes do happen more quickly in the microwave than on the stove, so close observation is needed during heating to ensure the fiber or yarn doesn't overheat.

Prepare to dye

Prepare the yarn or fiber for dyeing if desired (see pages 57-58). Measure out the dye powder and place it in a disposable cup. Dissolve the dye powder in very hot water. Pour the dissolved dye into your dyeing vessel. Add enough water to the vessel to cover the fiber, with a little extra for steam loss. Place the fiber or yarn in the bowl. Neatly arrange the fiber or yarn.

Heat dye bath

Cover the top of the vessel with plastic wrap. Place the covered dye bath in the microwave. Heat the dye bath until it just starts to boil. Allow the dye bath to rest for approximately 10 minutes, then heat it again until it just starts to boil. Anytime you hear a popping sound from the microwave, stop heating immediately and allow the dye bath to rest and cool for approximately 10 minutes (popping occurs when the yarn or fiber is overheating).

Check dye bath

After heating the dye bath 4 or 5 times, check the water with the white spoon before each heating session to see whether all of the dye has been absorbed. If the yarn or fiber has risen partially out of the dye bath when you check it, gently push it back down into the dye bath with your white spoon. If the water has color in it, continue to heat the dye bath. Keep the dye bath covered with plastic wrap whenever you are not checking on the process.

Finish dyeing

Once the water in the vessel is clear, the dye bath has exhausted. Cover the vessel with plastic wrap and allow the dye bath to cool to room temperature. Rinse and dry the dyed fiber or yarn (see page 70).

 Tip

During heating the steam may cause the plastic wrap to expand into a bubble on top of the vessel. As the vessel cools, the plastic wrap will start to droop. Do not let the plastic wrap droop enough to touch the yarn, fiber or dye bath. If this occurs, restretch the plastic wrap over the vessel so it does not droop, or replace it with a new piece. The plastic wrap can fuse to your yarn or fiber if you allow them to touch during heating. This will ruin your yarn or fiber.

Dyeing a Single Color in a Crockpot

Dyeing yarn or roving in a crockpot requires the least amount of babysitting, but it is also the most time-intensive dye method. This is a great dye choice when you're going to be around the house for a while but don't want to be stuck in the kitchen. The crockpot is a great choice for hard-to-set dyes as well, because it works at stubborn dyes with low, steady heat. The crockpot is the only place I can get rich, consistent results from black dye, which is notoriously stubborn. I have found that exhausting a dye bath in the crockpot takes approximately 2 hours.

Prepare to dye

Prepare the yarn or fiber for dyeing if desired (see pages 57–58). Measure out the dye powder and split it into several small cups or into one large cup. (I prefer small cups because I find it easier to control pouring the dye from them.) Add hot water to the cups and stir until the dye dissolves. Neatly arrange the yarn or fiber in the bottom of the crockpot. You can work in a spiral or lay out the yarn or fiber from side to side. If necessary, arrange the yarn or fiber in layers.

Add dye

Pour the dye over the yarn or fiber. Add just enough dye to cover the yarn or fiber. Place the lid on the crockpot and turn it on to the Low setting. Put the lid on the crockpot.

Check dye bath

Check on the dye bath every 20–30 minutes. If the dye bath has started bubbling vigorously, turn the crockpot to the Warm setting. Once the bubbling stops, you can turn it back to Low. Occasionally check the dye bath using a white spoon to see whether the yarn or fiber has absorbed the dye. If the dye bath still has color, allow the yarn or fiber to continue heating.

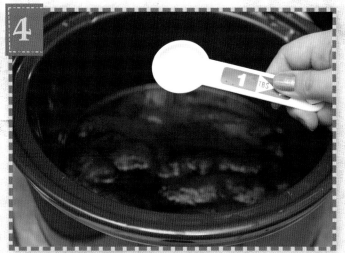

Complete dye process

Once the water in the crockpot is clear, the dye bath has exhausted. Put the lid on the crockpot and allow the dye bath to cool to room temperature. Rinse and dry the dyed fiber or yarn (see page 70).

Tip

In addition to slowly working away at stubborn dyes, the crockpot is also a great choice for creating very dark shades. I get the most consistent results for dark shades by using the crockpot.

Guidelines for Dyeing Multiple Colors by Stovetop, Microwave and Crockpot

While dyeing multiple colors by any of the methods provided in this book, you should follow these guidelines:

Dyes: For multicolor dyeing, the proportion of dye to liquid is as important as the proportion of dye to fiber because only a certain amount of liquid can be used. Using too much dye liquid will cause dye mixing, resulting in muddy colors. Just enough dye liquid should be added to the yarn or fiber to thoroughly wet it.

To determine how much dye liquid is needed, soak the yarn or fiber in a basin of water. Remove the yarn or fiber from the basin, then squeeze the excess water out into an empty basin. Measure the amount of water that comes out of the yarn or fiber. This is how much dye liquid the yarn or fiber can absorb. Divide that amount of liquid by the number of colors you plan to use. For instance, if your yarn or fiber absorbs 3 cups of water and you plan to use 3 colors, you will need 1 cup of dye liquid for each color (3 cups/3 colors = 1 cup per color).

Dissolve the dye powders in very hot water, each color in its own cup. The dye must be completely dissolved.

Placing yarn: Always neatly arrange the yarn or fiber in the dye vessel. You can work in a spiral or lay out the yarn or fiber from side to side. If necessary, arrange the yarn or fiber in layers.

Adding multiple dyes: Begin with the dye with the lightest value so it can stake its claim on the fiber. A darker dye can cover a lighter dye that spreads to the wrong area, but a light dye cannot cover a dark dye. Wear latex or rubber gloves and press the dye into the fiber or yarn so it is absorbed and does not shift to other parts of the dyepot. Gently add the next lightest color to the yarn or fiber, being careful not to let the second color run into the yarn or fiber covered with the first dye. You can leave white areas if you'd like, but make them much larger than you intend for the finished product because the dye will spread and cover some of the areas you leave white.

Heating the dye: Because there is so little liquid used in these processes, follow the heating directions for each method carefully to avoid overheating the fiber.

Checking the dye bath: Pulling a sample of the dye bath out in a white spoon is the easiest way to check the water for dye. If the water has color in it, continue to heat the dye bath. If the yarn or fiber rises partially out of the dye bath when you check it, gently push it back down into the dye bath with the white spoon.

Exhausting the dye bath: When the water in the pot is clear, the dye bath has exhausted, which means all of the dye has been absorbed by the yarn or fiber. This is the optimal situation in dyeing because it means that you are not wasting any dye and you know exactly how much dye is in the fiber, meaning you can replicate the results. For information on why a dye bath may not exhaust and how to handle those situations, see page 71.

Dyeing Multiple Colors on the Stovetop

While I recommend stovetop dyeing to beginners for a single color dye bath, I do not recommend the stovetop for multi-color dyeing. Because so little liquid is used, the fiber or yarn is very close to the heat source and can easily be burned. The only reason to dye multiple colors on the stovetop is because you don't have a microwave or crockpot that can be exclusively devoted to dyeing. Otherwise, the microwave and crockpot methods are easier and more likely to yield successful results.

Prepare to dye
Prepare the yarn or fiber for dyeing if desired (see pages 57–58). Dissolve the powder dye in very hot water. (To determine how much water you'll need, see Guidelines for Dyeing Multiple Colors on page 63.)

Arrange yarn or fiber
Neatly arrange the prepared yarn or fiber in the bottom of a nonreactive pot. You can work in a spiral or lay out the yarn or fiber from side to side. If necessary, arrange the yarn or fiber in layers.

Add dye
Carefully pour the first dye onto the fiber. Begin with the dye with the lightest value so it can stake its claim on the fiber. Wearing latex or rubber gloves, press the dye into the fiber or yarn so that it is absorbed and does not shift to other parts of the dye pot. Gently add the next lightest color to the yarn or fiber, being careful not to let the second color run into the yarn or fiber covered with the first dye.

Heat dye
Finish adding the remaining dyes until the fiber or yarn is covered as you desire. Gently heat the dye pot and monitor it very carefully so that the yarn or fiber does not burn. There will not be much excess liquid in the pot, but check it often to see if the dye bath is exhausting. Keep a lid on the pot between checks. Once the dye bath has exhausted, put the lid on the pot and allow the fiber or yarn to cool to room temperature. Rinse and dry the dyed fiber or yarn (see page 70).

Dyeing Multiple Colors in the Microwave

Dyeing multiple colors in the microwave can yield results as wild or as controlled as you want them to be. The fewer colors you use, the easier it is to control the results, but don't be afraid to experiment. Wide swaths of color on fiber will provide long color sections in spinning, and small dots will blend and mesh to form new colors when spun. Try laying out sock weight yarn from side to side in the dye vessel and adding dye from side to side, and you'll have self-striping sock yarn. A Pyrex casserole dish works well for this method of dyeing.

Prepare to dye

Prepare the yarn or fiber for dyeing if desired (see pages 57–58). Measure the amount of dye needed. (To determine how much water you'll need, see Guidelines for Dyeing Multiple Colors on page 63.) Mix as many or as few colors as you desire. (Here, I am using three colors.) Neatly arrange the yarn or fiber in the dye vessel. Begin with the dye with the lightest value. Press the dye into the fiber. Wear gloves when handling the dye-soaked yarn or fiber.

Continue adding dye

Add the next lightest dye to the yarn or fiber. Continue adding additional dyes until the yarn or fiber is covered as you desire. Only add enough dye to thoroughly wet the yarn or fiber.

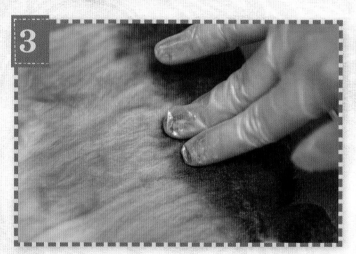

Finish adding dye

Add the dark dye to the fiber at least 1" (3cm) away from the light dye and push the dark dye through the yarn or fiber toward the light dye.

Heat dye

Cover the dye vessel with plastic wrap and place it in the microwave. Heat the dye-soaked yarn or fiber in short 1–2-minute bursts with 5 minute resting periods. Steam should form under the plastic wrap. Anytime you hear a popping sound from the microwave, stop heating immediately and allow the yarn or fiber to rest and cool. There will not be much excess liquid in the vessel, but check it after every 2 or 3 heating cycles to see if the dye bath is exhausting. Keep the vessel covered between checks. Once the dye bath has exhausted, cover the vessel and allow the yarn or fiber to cool to room temperature. Rinse and dry the dyed fiber or yarn (see page 70).

Tip

When adding darker dyes, start adding the dye away from the lighter color and work toward the lighter color; this will help you keep better control over the darker dye and keep it from covering the lighter dye colors.

Dyeing Multiple Colors in a Crockpot

Dyeing multiple colors in a crockpot has the same benefits as dyeing a single color in a crockpot: it's a simple, low maintenance method of dyeing. Because the process does take longer than dyeing multiple colors in the microwave, the dye has more time to spread and there is a greater risk of colors mixing and muddying, but this can be prevented with careful dye application.

Prepare to dye

Prepare the yarn or fiber for dyeing if desired (see pages 57–58). Mix as many or as few colors as you desire. Dissolve the dye powders completely in the required amount of very hot water. (To determine how much water you'll need, see Guidelines for Dyeing Multiple Colors on page 63.)

Arrange yarn or fiber

Neatly arrange the prepared yarn or fiber in the bottom of the crockpot. Carefully pour the first dye onto the fiber. Begin with the dye with the lightest value. Press the dye into the fiber or yarn.

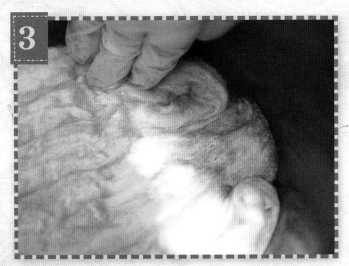

Continue adding dye

Gently add the next lightest color to the yarn or fiber, being careful not to let the second color run into the yarn or fiber covered with the first dye. Start adding the new dye color at least 1" (3cm) away from the lighter color and work toward the lighter color.

Heat dye

Finish adding the remaining dyes until the fiber or yarn is covered as you desire. Turn the crockpot on to Low until it starts steaming and then turn the heat down to Warm. Keep the heat on Warm to ensure that the yarn or fiber doesn't burn. After an hour, check approximately every 20 minutes to see if the dye bath is exhausting. Keep a lid on the crockpot between checks. Once the dye bath has exhausted, put the lid on the crockpot and allow the yarn or fiber to cool to room temperature. Rinse and dry the dyed fiber or yarn (see page 70).

Hand-Painting Roving

Hand-painting roving and yarn is the most precise and controlled method of dye application. It uses the least amount of liquid, so there's the least chance of accidental dye blending. And in spite of being the most controlled and precise, I think it also allows the most room for creativity. You can use more colors with hand painting because you have the entire length of the roving to play with instead of small areas in a dye pot or vessel. If you like "happy accidents" when it comes to creative play, this may not be the method for you, but if you want to know what you're going to get in the end, try hand painting.

Prepare to dye

Prepare the yarn or fiber for dyeing if desired (see pages 57–58). Measure the amount of dye needed. (To determine how much water you'll need, see Guidelines for Dyeing Multiple Colors on page 63.) Mix as many or as few colors as you desire. Dissolve the dye powders completely in the required amount of very hot water. If you are working in an area you want to protect from dye, lay out a plastic tablecloth to work on. Lay out a piece of plastic wrap approximately 18" (46cm) longer than the roving or skein of yarn you are dyeing. Spread out the yarn or roving on top of the plastic wrap with approximately 9" (23cm) of excess plastic wrap on each end. Choose the tools you'd like to apply the dye with: large, soft-bristled paintbrushes; squirt bottles; or sponge brushes.

Begin painting

Once your work area is set up, begin painting the yarn or fiber.

If you are using paintbrushes or sponge brushes: Dip the brush in the dye and then transfer the dye to the yarn or fiber with an up-and-down dabbing motion, like you are poking the yarn or fiber. Do not move the brush back and forth along the yarn or roving like you are painting a wall; this will disturb the fiber structure of top or roving and will also leave a skein of yarn in disarray. Try to work with as few dabs as possible—excessive dabbing can work like a felting needle and felt the yarn or fiber. For full coverage, saturate the fiber or yarn with dye. For mottled, semisolid areas, vary the amount of dye over each section.

If you are applying dye with a squirt bottle: Squirt the dye onto the fiber or yarn, and then press the dyed area with your fingers so that the fiber or yarn completely absorbs the dye.

Tip

A variety of color effects can be achieved with hand painting. In the example above I am making the painted areas the same length for each color, but you can paint your yarn or fiber however you desire. You can paint long areas of a main color with short bursts of complementary colors, or sprinkle dye over the yarn or roving for tiny dots of color. You can also leave some areas unpainted.

When painting fiber, it is useful to know the staple length of the fiber you are dyeing (see Preparing Fiber for Spindle or Wheel on page 23). If you want clear, unmuddied colors, each section of dye must be longer than the staple length. Having dyed areas shorter than the fiber's staple length will cause the colors of the fiber to blend during spinning. The longer a color section is in the yarn or fiber, the longer that color section will appear in spinning, knitting or weaving.

Dealing with adjacent colors

When two colors are adjacent to each other on the yarn or roving, you can choose to blend them together to form a gradual color shift, or you can keep them apart for distinct color changes.

If you want to prevent blending: Start by painting with the new color at least 1" (3cm) away from the previous color. Slowly and carefully work the new color toward the old color.

To completely prevent blending: Leave a very small white space between the two colors. This small white space will show up in the finished product when you are dyeing yarn but it will be nearly invisible in fiber because it will blend into the other colors during spinning.

To blend colors: Paint the same area with both dyes.

Paint reverse side

Once the length of fiber or yarn is painted as you desire, carefully turn it over on the plastic wrap and check for places where the dye did not soak through. It is common to have white areas on the bottom of the fiber or yarn. If there are any white areas, paint them with the appropriate color of dye.

Wrap fiber or yarn

Once the fiber or yarn is painted as you desire, fold the plastic wrap over the fiber or yarn, first on one side, then on the other. Make sure the fiber or yarn is completely and snugly encased in plastic wrap.

Roll fiber or yarn

Start at one end and roll up the painted fiber or yarn in a spiral like a cinnamon roll. Seal the excess plastic wrap at each end of the roll so dye cannot escape.

Tip

Some color blends can be quite appealing, while others are not as attractive. Complementary colors, or colors that are opposite each other on the color wheel, form brown when blended.

Setting Hand–Painted Dye on the Stovetop

I prefer to set the dye in hand–painted rovings on the stovetop. The temperature is easy to control and the heating is even, providing an even color in the finished product. If you are going to steam the hand–painted yarn or roving on the stovetop, the yarn or roving must be kept out of the boiling water and exposed to steam only. Some pots come with a steamer basket. If the lid will not fit when the painted yarn is placed in the steamer basket, or if your pot does not have its own steamer insert, you can purchase a vegetable steamer basket and elevate it out of the boiling water, as I show you here.

Set up steamer for stovetop heating

Use a large Pyrex measuring cup turned upside down in the bottom of the pot to elevate the steamer basket. The setup is shown here out of the pot. Place the painted fiber in the steamer basket on top of the Pyrex measuring cup.

Set dye on the stovetop

Bring a pot of water to a boil, and then place the painted yarn or fiber in the pot so it is exposed to the steam, but not the water. Keep a lid on the pot to capture the steam and evenly heat the dyed material. After 10 minutes, use a pair of tongs to turn over the dyed material. Allow it to steam an additional 10 minutes. Remove the dyed material from the pot and allow the yarn or fiber to cool to room temperature. Remove the plastic wrap from the yarn or fiber. Rinse and dry the dyed fiber or yarn (see page 70).

Setting Hand–Painted Dye in the Microwave

It is possible to set the dye in hand–painted fiber or yarn in the microwave, but careful monitoring is needed to ensure even heating and, therefore, even dye setting.

Set dye in the microwave

Place the rolled-up dye material in a microwave-safe dish to contain any dye that leaks from the roll. Heat the yarn or fiber in short 1–2 minute bursts with 5-minute resting periods. Steam should form in the plastic wrap, causing the roll to puff up. Anytime you hear a popping sound from the microwave, stop heating immediately and allow the yarn or fiber to rest and cool. Popping occurs when the yarn or fiber is overheating. After 2 or 3 heating sessions, turn the roll over with tongs and continue the pattern of heating and resting. After 8 or 9 heating sessions, allow the yarn or fiber to cool to room temperature. Remove the plastic wrap from the yarn or fiber. Rinse and dry the dyed fiber or yarn (see page 70).

Rinsing and Drying Dyed Fiber or Yarn

One more step to go and your dyed creation will be ready to use. Once the dye bath has exhausted, or once you are satisfied with the dyed material, it is time to rinse and dry the fiber or yarn. After that, your lovely fiber or yarn will be ready to work with!

Test rinse water
For best results, I recommend waiting until the dyed fiber or yarn has cooled to room temperature and rinsing in water that is also room temperature. It gives the yarn or fiber a little more time to absorb dye, and it also helps prevent felting. However, if you are just too impatient and/or excited to wait until the dye bath has cooled completely, make the rinse water the same temperature as the dye bath. Here, I am testing the rinse water to make sure it matches the temperature of the dye bath, which has not yet cooled to room temperature.

Press out excess water
Wearing gloves if the water is hot or if there is still dye in the dye bath, remove the fiber or yarn from the dye bath. Squeeze the excess dye liquid out of the fiber or yarn. Be careful not to wring or agitate the fibers or yarn too much or they may felt.

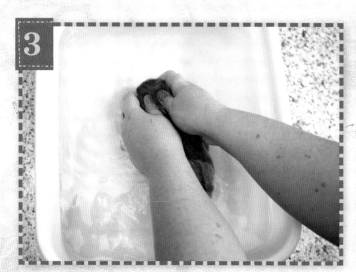

Rinse fiber or yarn
Place the yarn or fiber on the surface of the rinse water and let it sink into the water. Allow the yarn or fiber to soak for a few minutes. Gently squeeze along the length of the yarn or fiber to release any excess dye. Repeat in fresh rinse water until the water runs clear. Do not wring or excessively agitate the yarn or fiber, and do not change the temperature of the rinse water between rinses—these things may cause felting.

Dry fiber or yarn
Remove the yarn or fiber from the final rinse bath. Squeeze the excess water out of the fiber or yarn. A clean, dry towel can be used to press excess water out of yarn, but not fiber. Lay the yarn or fiber flat on a nonabsorbent surface, or hang the yarn or fiber to dry. When hanging, the yarn or fiber may drip at first, so hang it over a surface that won't be damaged by water. To prevent dripping, lay the fiber or yarn flat to dry.

Exhausting a Dye Bath

As stated earlier, it is best to exhaust a dye bath. When a dye bath exhausts, no dye is wasted and you know exactly how much dye it took to produce a certain color. However, a dye bath may not always exhaust. Fiber and yarn can only absorb a certain amount of dye, so if there is more dye in the pot than the fiber or yarn can absorb, the dye bath will never exhaust. Some dye colors are very stubborn about setting and are therefore very difficult to exhaust. Or you may reach the color you desire before the dye is exhausted. Also, you may run out of time or patience before a dye bath is able to exhaust. This is another reason I recommend letting dyed fiber or yarn return to room temperature before removing it from the dye bath. Quite a bit of dye can be absorbed by cooling yarn or fiber. If your dye bath does not exhaust, instead of throwing the dye out, you can add more undyed fiber or yarn to absorb the remaining dye. This is a great way to get pastel colors, and I've achieved many "happy accident" colors this way.

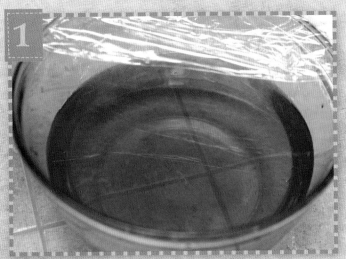

Cool dye bath
If you did not allow the dye bath to cool to room temperature with the dyed yarn or fiber in it, allow it to cool to room temperature before adding more yarn or fiber. Adding fiber or yarn to a hot dye bath can cause felting.

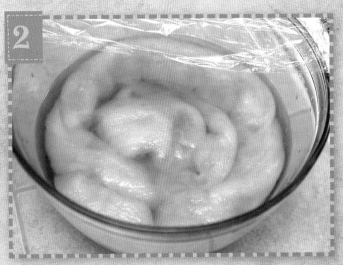

Add yarn or fiber
Prepare the yarn or fiber for dyeing if desired (see pages 57–58). Neatly arrange the fiber or yarn in the dye vessel for even dyeing results. If the dye bath does not completely cover the yarn or fiber, push the yarn or fiber to the side of the pot and add more water to the side without fiber or yarn. Do not pour water directly on the fiber or it may felt.

Exhaust dye bath
Follow the heating instructions for your chosen method of dyeing (see Dyeing a Single Color on the Stovetop on page 60, Dyeing a Single Color in the Microwave on page 61 or Dyeing a Single Color in a Crockpot on page 62). Heat the dye bath until the dye bath is exhausted.

STITCH

Once you've begun spinning and dyeing, you will start accumulating handspun yarn. Unless your crafting goal is to create an art installation titled "Baskets of Yarn," you'll probably want to start making some projects using your handmade yarn. However, those first skeins of yarn you make may be difficult to work into patterns written for commercial yarns. That's because commercial yarns don't have the special "design features" of handspun yarn, like lumps, bumps, thin spots and overall character. There's also the fact that you're probably not going to spin a sweater's worth of yarn right out of the spinning gate, so you'll need small projects to use your special yarns.

This chapter features ten projects designed for handspun yarn. From small projects that use only a few yards of handspun like the *Drop Stitch Scarf* on page 76, to the big, cozy *Lap Blanket* on page 84 with tons of handspun charm, there's a project for whatever amount of yarn you've created. The projects also use a wide variety of yarns, from your lumpiest, bumpiest beginner yarns, to the more refined yarns you can create with a bit of practice. Most of these projects also feature a combination of handspun yarns and commercial yarns so you can get the most mileage from your handspun. If you'd like to create any of these projects exclusively in handspun yarn, feel free to substitute a handspun yarn in the same gauge as the commercial yarn used in the project.

Wristers

These wristers use just a little bit of yarn in a big way! The Stockinette stitch body is a great way to show off the beautiful colors of your latest skein of handspun yarn, while the ribbed cuffs give you a perfect fit without a lot of fuss. A few simple knitting techniques are all you need to turn your yarn into a pretty and practical winter (or chilly office) accessory. Because these are worn right next to the skin, I recommend starting with a soft fiber, such as Merino wool. For a cozy, dense fabric, spin a fairly smooth and even yarn. That way, you'll have wristers with no gaps or holes.

Project Information

SIZES
Women's average

FINISHED MEASUREMENTS
7" (18cm) at cuff, unstretched

YARN
70 yds (63m) 2-ply handspun, approx 9 wpi

NEEDLES
5 size US 8 (5mm) DPNs

NOTIONS
stitch marker
yarn needle

GAUGE
16 sts and 26 rows = 4" (10cm) in St st

NOTE
Piece is knit from the top down.

Pattern (Make 2)

CO 28 sts. Place marker and join for working the round, being careful not to twist sts. Work in k2, p2 rib for 1" (3cm).

Knit 2 rnds. At end of second rnd, turn and purl back. Work flat in St st until piece measures 3" (8cm) from cast-on edge for thumb opening.

Resume working in the round in St st until piece measures 5½" (14cm) from cast-on edge.

Work in k2, p2 rib for 1" (3cm) more. BO.

FINISHING
Weave in ends.

Drop Stitch Scarf

This clever scarf is the perfect way to show off those first lumpy, bumpy yarns you make. Because the body of the scarf is knit with commercial yarn and then embellished with handspun, you only need a few yards of handspun yarn to finish this project. And the way the handspun yarn is used is very forgiving of those beginner "design features" that some might call imperfections. Knit the scarf, drop a few stitches to form a ladder, and presto! You have the perfect place to showcase a bit of unique yarn.

Pattern

Seed Stitch Rib
Row 1 (RS): K3, p1, k5, p1, k5, p1, k3.
Row 2: Purl.
Rep Rows 1 & 2 for patt.

SCARF
With MC, CO 19 sts.
Work in Seed Stitch Rib patt until piece measures 72" (183cm) from cast-on edge, ending with a WS row.

Next row (RS): BO 6 sts in patt. Drop the next st. BO the following st very loosely, then BO the next 4 sts in patt. Drop the next st. BO the following st very loosely, then BO the next 5 sts in patt.

FINISHING
Unravel the 2 dropped sts down to the CO row.

Weave in ends. Wash and block the scarf. Allow the scarf to dry completely. Cut six 90" (229cm) lengths of CC. Weave 3 strands of yarn through each dropped stitch ladder. Knot the strands tog on each end of the scarf.

Cut sixty-eight 16" (41cm) strands of MC for fringe. To attach the fringe, fold two strands of yarn in half tog, place the crochet hook through the edge of the scarf and pull the looped ends of the yarn through the knitted fabric. Thread the yarn tails through the looped ends, then pull the yarn tails to tighten. Rep seventeen times on each end of the scarf. Trim the ends even.

Project Information

SIZES
One size

FINISHED MEASUREMENTS
4½" x 72" (11cm x 183cm) excluding fringe

YARN
2 skeins Cascade 220 (100% wool, 220 yds [201m] per 100g skein) in color #8555 Black (MC)
15 yds (14m) thick-and-thin 2-ply handspun, approx 6 wpi (CC)

NEEDLES
size US 7 (4.5mm) straight needles

NOTIONS
size US G-7 (4.5mm) crochet hook
yarn needle

GAUGE
20 sts and 26 rows = 4" (10cm) in patt st

NOTE
Scarf width will increase slightly after handspun is woven in.

Dropping a Stitch

In most knitting projects, you want to avoid dropped stitches, but they're not always a bad thing. In fact, a dropped stitch can make a great decorative element in a knitted project. Follow these easy steps, and enjoy a little knitting anarchy.

1

Slip stitch off needle
Bind off as usual to the stitch that will be dropped. Slip the stitch off of the left needle.

2

Bind off next stitch
Tug on the loop on the right needle to make it approximately three times as long as you would for a normal bind off stitch. Bind off the next stitch on the left needle.

3

Begin dropping stitch
Finish binding off following the pattern, dropping stitches where indicated. Once the edge is completely bound off, go to the first dropped stitch along the bound-off edge. Tug on the fabric on either side of the dropped stitch. The knitted loops will start to pop out of each other, traveling downward toward the cast-on edge. Moderate tugging ought to be enough to keep the stitch running, but if the stitch gets stuck on a stubborn loop, you can use the point of a knitting needle to poke the loops apart.

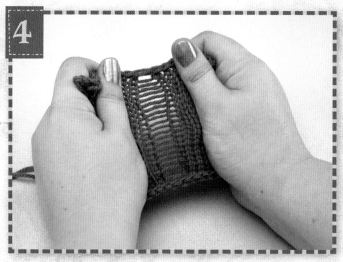

4

Finish dropping stitch
Continue tugging and prodding the dropped stitch until it unravels all the way down to the cast-on edge. Repeat Steps 3–4 with all dropped stitches.

Pick up bars

Thread your decorative yarn on a yarn needle. Weave the needle through the horizontal bars of the drop stitch ladder, going over three bars and under one.

Pull yarn through

Use the needle to draw the yarn through the horizontal bars of the drop stitch ladder. You may need to tug back and forth on the ends of the decorative yarn to make it lay nicely in the drop stitch ladder. If you're using more than one strand, use your fingers or the tip of the yarn needle to nudge the yarn to one side of the ladder to make room for more strands.

One Way or Another Hat

This hat doesn't know which way it's going! With a brim knit perpendicular to the crown, this hat features a unique construction for your unique yarns. And even though the construction isn't the norm, this hat is still quite easy to make and very fun to wear, with its big, cheerful, handspun pom-pom. I recommend a fairly even yarn for the brim for warmth, but the pom-pom can display your wildest handspun creation without sacrificing comfort.

Make It Your Own

A fairly even yarn for the brim of this hat will keep your head warmer because the fabric made from it won't have any holes or gaps. I also recommend spinning the yarn for your brim from a soft fiber—your forehead will thank you. However, while you're considering those things for the brim yarn, you can use the pom-pom to display your handspun creation featuring a funky color or unusual fiber. I do suggest a plied yarn if you want a puffy, rounded pom-pom; a singles yarn that isn't perfectly balanced will twist back on itself, making your pom-pom look spiky (and if that's what you want, go for it!).

Project Information

SIZES
Women's average

FINISHED MEASUREMENTS
19" (48cm) at brim, unstretched

YARN
1 skein Cascade 220 (wool, 220 yds [201m] per 100g skein) in color #8887 Dark Lavender (MC)
27 yds (24m) coordinating 2-ply handspun, approx 6 wpi (CC)

NEEDLES
size US 10 ½ (6.5mm) straight needles
16" (41cm) size US 6 (4mm) circular needle
5 size US 6 (4mm) DPNs

NOTIONS
stitch markers
yarn needle
4" × 6" (10cm × 15cm) piece of sturdy cardboard

GAUGE
14 sts and 14 rows = 4" (10cm) in garter st using CC and larger needles
20 sts and 28 rows = 4" (10cm) in St st using MC and smaller needles

Pattern

With larger needles and CC, CO 6 sts. Work in garter st for 19½" (50cm). BO. Join CO and BO edges tog using mattress stitch.

With circular needle and MC, pick up and knit 99 sts along the long edge of the handspun brim. Place marker and join in a rnd. Work even in St st until piece measures 5½" (14cm) from bottom of brim.

Next rnd: *K9, k2tog, pm; rep from * around—90 sts.
Next rnd: Knit.
Next rnd: *Knit to 2 sts before marker, k2tog; rep from * around—81 sts.
Rep last 2 rnds eight times more—9 sts.
Next row: K1, *k2tog; rep from * around—5 sts.
Cut yarn, leaving an 8" (20cm) tail. Thread the tail through rem sts, pull tight and fasten off.

FINISHING
Weave in ends.
Create a loopy pom-pom as directed on page 83. Attach it to the top of the hat with the strands of MC.

Making a Pom-Pom

Pom-poms make a cute addition to any number of projects. From the tip of a hat to the top of a simple slipper, pom-poms add a touch of cozy fun.

Wrap leftover CC around board
Wrap the remaining CC around a 4" x 6" (10cm x 15cm) piece of sturdy cardboard.

Slide yarn off cardboard
Lay out an 8" (20cm) strand of MC. Slide the yarn bundle off the cardboard on top of the strand of MC.

Secure yarn bundle
Tie the yarn bundle around the middle using the strand of MC. Secure the bundle with a knot.

Finish pom-pom
Using your fingers, fluff the pom-pom. Attach the pom-pom to the item using the piece of MC.

Lap Blanket

This project is for someone who's been bitten hard by the spinning bug. It uses quite a bit of yardage, but it's worth it in the end because there's nothing like being surrounded by your own lovely yarns. To cut down on the amount of handspun used in the blanket, you can make more than half the blocks from commercial yarn. You can also go whole hog and spin yarn for the entire blanket. This blanket is also easy to resize—just make more or fewer blocks for a custom fit.

Pattern

Basketweave Blocks (Make six)
With yarn A and larger needles, cast on 66 sts.
Rows 1–9: K9, [p8, k8] three times, p9.
Rows 10–18: P9, [k8, p8] three times, k9.
Rep Rows 1–18 three times more. BO.

Stockinette Blocks (Make six)
With B and smaller needles, CO 72 sts.
Work in St st until piece measures 14½" (37cm) from beg. BO.

FINISHING
Wash and block blocks to 14½" x 14½" (37cm x 37cm). Allow blocks to dry completely. Arrange blocks as desired in four rows of three blocks each. Join blocks into strips with single crochet, using the crochet hook and A. Join strips in the same fashion. Join A at the outside edge of the blanket and work 1 rnd single crochet, fasten off. Weave in ends.

Project Information

SIZES
One size

FINISHED MEASUREMENTS
44" x 58" (112cm x 147cm)

YARN
8 skeins Elann Peruvian Highland Wool (wool, 109 yds [100m] per 50g skein); 2 skeins in each of four colors (A) or as desired (see Note for additional information)
As shown, blanket uses #0743 Grape Heather, #0616 Redwood, #0683 Chestnut and #0620 Garnet.
750 yds (686m) 2-ply handspun, approx 9.5 wpi (B)
As shown, blanket uses three colors of handspun, 750 yds (686m) total.

NEEDLES
size US 7 (4.5mm) straight needles
size US 8 (5mm) straight needles

NOTIONS
size US H-8 (5mm) crochet hook
yarn needle

GAUGE
18 sts and 20 rows = 4" (10cm) in Basketweave patt using A and larger needles
20 sts and 26 rows = 4" (10cm) in St st using B and smaller needles

NOTE
Each Basketweave block in this blanket uses 1⅓ skeins of yarn. If you are using one or two colors for the Basketweave blocks, 8 skeins of yarn will be enough to finish the blanket. If you are using more than two colors, calculate your yarn needs by multiplying the number of blocks you plan for each color by 1⅓. Round this number up to the nearest whole number for the number of skeins you need for that color. For example, if you want two purple squares, you'll need 3 skeins of purple yarn (2 x 1⅓ = 2⅔, round up to 3).

Ear Warmer

Weaving is a technique that is very forgiving to uneven yarns. This project takes full advantage of that fact, turning a thick-and-thin bulky yarn into thick, cushy fabric that is very warm and snuggly. Tie this ear warmer at the nape of your neck for a convenient headband that will keep your ears warm without squashing your hair, or try tying it under your chin for an adorable bonnet look. Either way, you'll keep toasty warm in your own handspun yarn.

Instructions

Cut ten 34" (86cm) pieces of yarn B and six pieces of yarn A. To warp the loom, begin by tying a knot 5" (13cm) from one end of each piece of cut yarn. Secure the knots to the cardboard with straight pins, separated by a space as wide as a piece of yarn (see Warping on pins on page 88). Stretch the first piece of yarn, measure it against the loom and tie a knot in the yarn even with the opposite edge of the loom. Secure the knot to the cardboard with a straight pin. Repeat with every length of warp yarn.

*Measure off 2 yds (2m) of yarn B and form a weaving butterfly with it (see Managing Weaving Yarn on page 89). Weave for 1¾" (4cm) (see Begin Weaving on page 89). Measure off two 2-yd (2m) strands of yarn A and wind both strands into a weaving butterfly together. Weave for 1¾" (4cm). Repeat from * three more times. Weave one more section of yarn B.

Unpin all warp strands from the loom. Knot the first two warp strands together with a square knot. Repeat with the next two warp ends and across all warp ends. Wash and block the ear warmer. Braid the warp ends to form ties at each end of the ear warmer.

Project Information

YARN

1 skein Lion Brand Homespun (98% acrylic/2% polyester, 185 yds [169m] per 170g skein) (A)
20 yds (18m) 2-ply handspun, approx 5 wpi (B)

MATERIALS

7" × 24" (18cm × 61cm) piece of sturdy cardboard
straight pins
yarn needle

Simple Weaving

Weaving, like knitting, is a way to organize yarn into fabric. Weaving is a grid made of vertical strands, called warp, and horizontal strands, called weft. Large pieces of fabric are usually created on looms, but you can come up with all kinds of ingenious ways to make small pieces of fabric with supplies you probably already have around your home. The woven projects in this book were all created on pieces of sturdy cardboard with pins or binder clips to hold the warp in place. These easy steps will have you weaving in no time.

Warping the Loom: Choose one

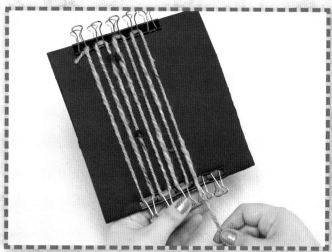

Warping on bulldog clips

Attach small bulldog clips side by side to two opposing sides of the cardboard "loom." Secure the warp yarn to the first clip with a knot. Wrap the yarn evenly and tightly across the loom and around the bulldog clip opposite the first. Wrap the yarn evenly and tightly up to the second clip on the opposite side. Repeat across all the bulldog clips. Cut the yarn, and tie it to the last bulldog clip.

Warping on pins

Cut all of the strands of warp yarn approximately 10" (25cm) longer than your loom. Tie a knot 5" (13cm) from one end of each piece of cut yarn. Secure the knots to the cardboard with the straight pins, separated by a space as wide as a piece of yarn. Stretch the first piece of yarn, measure it against the loom and tie a knot in the yarn even with the opposite edge of the loom. Secure the knot to the cardboard with a straight pin. Repeat with every length of warp yarn.

Warping around cardboard

Tie a knot in one end of the warp yarn. Secure the knot to the cardboard with a straight pin. Wrap the yarn evenly and tightly around the cardboard "loom," leaving a gap the width of a strand of warp yarn between each wrap. Cut the yarn, tie a knot in the tail and secure it to the cardboard with a straight pin.

Managing Weaving Yarn

Wind yarn into butterfly
To organize the weft yarn, stretch out the fingers of one hand. Wrap the yarn around the pinkie finger and thumb in a figure eight.

Secure yarn
Once you've wound the amount of yarn you desire, slide it off of your hand. Wrap the yarn tail several times around the yarn where it crosses. Tuck the yarn tail under itself to secure it.

Draw out yarn
To draw yarn out of the weaving butterfly, gently pull on the end that is not secured. The yarn should draw out smoothly without tangling.

Begin Weaving

Weave first weft strand
Use a thin dpn or crochet hook to lift every other warp strand. If you are weaving a piece of fabric that is more than 2" (5cm) wide, you may need to work a few strands at a time. Slip the end of the weft yarn under the lifted warp strands and over the unlifted warp strands. Work the weft strand all the way across the warp. Pull the weft yarn through the warp so that there is a piece of weft to the side of the warp as long as the warp is wide, plus 2" (5cm) (for example, if the warp was 4" [10cm], you would leave a 6" [15cm] tail of weft on the side of the warp).

Weave second weft strand
Lift the same warp strands again and pass the weaving butterfly under the lifted strands and over the unlifted strands. Work the weaving butterfly all the way across the warp as well. Leave a loop of yarn on the side of the warp opposite the weft tail and weaving butterfly.

Begin securing first weft end

Working between the two weft strands, use your dpn or crochet hook to lift the warp ends that are under the weft yarn strands. Slip the excess tail of weft yarn under the lifted warp strands and over the unlifted warp strands. Work the weft tail all the way across the warp. Gently pull on the weft tail until it is just looped around the first warp strand.

Finish securing first weft end

Hold onto the short tail of weft yarn that is in the loop on the right of the warp. Gently pull on the weaving butterfly to tighten the weft yarn around the weft tail.

Compress weft

Use the tip of the dpn or crochet hook to push the weft strands together. They should rest against each other but not be crushed together. Work across the loom until the three strands are aligned.

Maintain selvedges

Every few rows of weft, pull on the outer warp strands to spread the weft at the edges. The edges of a piece of woven cloth are called the selvedges. It's very easy to pull the weft too tight, pulling in the selvedges. If you accidentally pull in a bit with each row, you'll eventually have a woven triangle instead of a square or rectangle. For neat, even edges, you need to tug on the edges occasionally to straighten them.

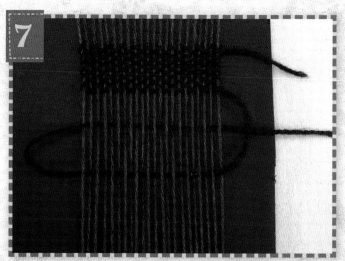

Begin securing last weft strand

When your woven cloth is the length you desire, weave two rows that go under the same warp strands instead of alternating. Leave a wide space between the two strands. Pick up the opposing strands between the two rows just woven and work the weaving butterfly through.

Finish securing last weft strand

Press the last three strands of weft together with the rest of the woven fabric. Gently pull each strand snug with the selvedges. Secure the last weft strand in the loop formed by the two previous rows.

Remove yarn from loom

If you've warped your loom with bulldog clips or straight pins, you can simply remove them to release your warp. If you've wrapped the loom, cut the warp at each edge of the loom.

Secure warp ends

Secure the edges of the fabric by tying the warp strands together with square knots. Start with the first two warp edges, then the next two and so on until all of the warp strands have been knotted. Repeat on each end.

Woven Pouch

This little project is the perfect way to take a little bit of your handspun with you wherever you go. Like other weaving projects, this one is very forgiving of lumps and bumps, and it's a great way to display a special bit of yarn. When weaving, the yarn used for the warp must be quite strong, so if your handspun is not up to the task, feel free to substitute commercial yarn for the warp and save your precious handspun for the weft. You'll get more mileage out of just a few yards of yarn that way.

Make It Your Own

To create yarn that is strong enough for warp, try adding extra twist, both in the singles and when plying. Yarns with a lot of twist can feel hard or rough, something that isn't valued in a cozy scarf, but for a woven pouch it's actually a good thing. Highly twisted yarn can stand up to a lot more wear and tear than softly twisted yarns. Don't go overboard and add so much twist that the yarn corkscrews or snaps from the tension, but adding some extra twist to your yarn will make it perfect for items that need to take a little extra wear and tear.

Project Information

YARN
12 yds (11m) 2-ply thick-and-thin handspun, approx 6 wpi

MATERIALS
6" × 12" (15cm × 30cm) piece of sturdy cardboard
13 small bulldog clips
yarn needle
fabric for lining
thread and needle
button
snap

Instructions

To warp the loom, attach seven small bulldog clips side by side at one end of the loom and six on the opposite side (see Warping on bulldog clips on page 88). Secure the yarn to the first clip on the seven-clip side with a knot. Wrap the yarn evenly and tightly across the loom and around the bulldog clip opposite the first. Wrap the yarn evenly and tightly up to the second clip on the seven-clip side. Repeat across all the bulldog clips (warp ends). Cut the yarn, and tie it to the last bulldog clip.

Form a weaving butterfly with the remaining yarn. Weave for 9" (23cm) (see Managing Weaving Yarn and Begin Weaving on page 89).

Cut the excess warp yarn at each bulldog clip. Knot the first two warp strands together with a square knot. Repeat across all warp ends. Wash and block the woven fabric. Fold the fabric up 3" (8cm) from the bottom edge and sew both sides to form a pouch with a flap. Make a pouch with a flap in the same size from the lining fabric and sew the lining into the woven pouch. Make sure to tuck the excess warp ends under the lining as you sew. Sew the snap to the pouch. Disguise the snap stitching on the public side by sewing a button over the stitching.

94

Sewing in a Lining and a Snap

Once you've made the pouch, you'll want to make it more secure for your stuff by adding a lining and a snap closure. Lining a woven item is an easy way to hide the warp tails without a lot of effort. A lining also helps lengthen the life of your handspun by taking some of the wear and tear from whatever you keep inside the pouch. Small items can also slip between the strands in a coarse weave like this, so a lining and a snap keep everything safe and secure inside.

Turn lining under
Tuck the lining pouch into the woven pouch. Finger press the edges of the lining under for a neat, folded edge.

Sew in lining
Sew the lining to the pouch with small, neat stitches. Sew around the flap as well as the opening of the pouch.

Attach snap
Attach the first piece of the snap just below the opening of the pouch. Fold the flap over, mark the location where the flap meets the snap with a pin, and then sew the second half of the snap to the flap of the pouch.

Mug Rugs

These cute little coasters are a quick and easy project to make, and they are a great way to show off some of your handspun yarn in your home décor. If you think your coasters will get a lot of wear and tear, you may want to consider using superwash wool as your spinning fiber. Superwash wool has been specially treated so that it can be washed without felting. You'll also need to use a fairly even yarn for this project so that the drinks set on the mug rugs won't be off balance due to lumps and bumps.

Project Information

YARN
55 yds (50m) 2-ply handspun, approx 9 wpi

MATERIALS
6½" × 7" (17cm × 18cm) piece of sturdy cardboard
straight pins

Instructions

To warp the loom, begin by tying a knot in one end of the yarn. Secure the knot to the cardboard with a straight pin. Wrap the yarn evenly and tightly around the loom 33 times over 4½" (11cm), parallel to the long side of the cardboard (see Warping around cardboard on page 88). Cut the yarn, tie a knot in the tail and secure to the cardboard with a straight pin.

Measure off 9 yds (8m) of yarn and form a weaving butterfly with it (see Managing Weaving Yarn on page 89). Weave for 4¼" (11cm) (see Begin Weaving on page 89). Repeat on the other side of the loom for a second coaster.

Cut the excess warp yarn between the two coasters on each side of the cardboard. Knot the first two warp strands together with a square knot. Repeat across all warp ends. Wash and block the coasters.

Handspun Wreath

This lovely project is a fun way to show off your handspun yarns, and you won't need to learn any special techniques. The wreath shown here is made with Christmas colors, but a wreath like this is a great addition to your home décor any time of the year. Try rich reds, oranges and yellows for an autumnal theme, or sweet pastels for a wreath reminiscent of spring. Or use up colorful odds and ends of yarn left after other projects for a bright, cheerful year-round decoration.

Make It Your Own

This is another project that is great for yarns that are too wild, lumpy or bumpy to create a smooth, wearable fabric. Whether you're making art yarns on purpose or by accident, in your spinning career you'll probably make at least one yarn that you absolutely love and absolutely can't find a use for. Here's a way you can use it and enjoy it—it will be on display for your viewing pleasure.

Project Information

YARN
60 yds (55m) thick-and-thin 2-ply handspun, approx 4–6 wpi, 10 yds (9m) in each of 6 colors (here I've used wine, maroon, red, tartan, pine and kelly green)
2 10-yd (9m) lengths cream thick-and-thin 2-ply handspun, approx 4–6 wpi

MATERIALS
12" (30cm) straw wreath
straight pins
craft felt in 3 colors (I used green, red and dark red)
small craft poms
craft glue
needle
thread

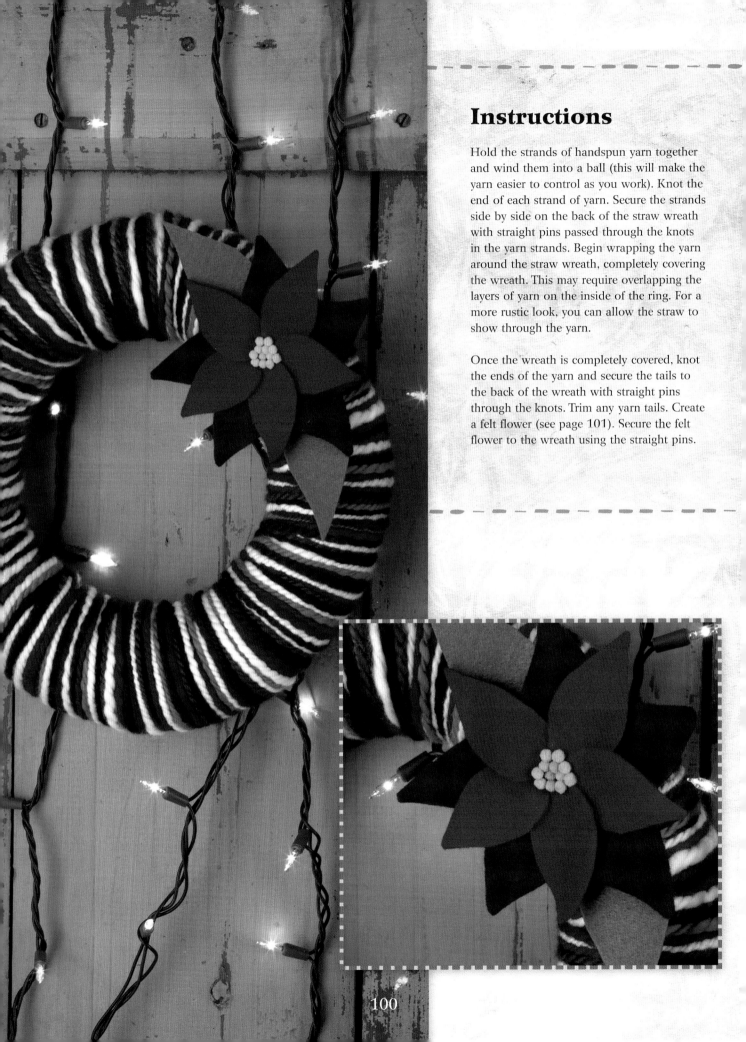

Instructions

Hold the strands of handspun yarn together and wind them into a ball (this will make the yarn easier to control as you work). Knot the end of each strand of yarn. Secure the strands side by side on the back of the straw wreath with straight pins passed through the knots in the yarn strands. Begin wrapping the yarn around the straw wreath, completely covering the wreath. This may require overlapping the layers of yarn on the inside of the ring. For a more rustic look, you can allow the straw to show through the yarn.

Once the wreath is completely covered, knot the ends of the yarn and secure the tails to the back of the wreath with straight pins through the knots. Trim any yarn tails. Create a felt flower (see page 101). Secure the felt flower to the wreath using the straight pins.

Creating a Felt Flower

This sweet felt flower makes a great embellishment for your wreath. Done in reds and greens, it resembles a poinsettia, but like the wreath, it can be altered to match a different seasonal theme. Add extra layers of petals to make a fall mum, or use spring or summer hues as you wish.

Assemble petals

Use the leaf template below to cut 10 flower petals from the craft felt, five each in two colors. Cut a 1½" x 1½" (4cm x 4cm) square of craft felt. Arrange the petals in a flower shape, centered over the square. Sew the petals to the square to secure them.

Glue craft poms

Dab glue in the center of the felt petals and place the craft poms in the glue. Allow the glue to dry completely.

Secure decoration to wreath

Use the leaf template to cut two leaves from the green craft felt. Experiment with the placement of the leaves and flower on the wreath. When you've found a position you like, tack the leaves to the wreath with straight pins. Lift the flower petals and secure the flower to the wreath by putting straight pins through the square base of the flower.

Leaf pattern

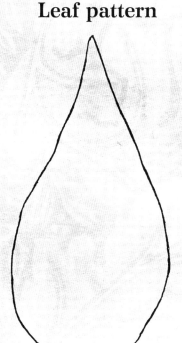

Couched Embroidery Scarf

Even one yard of handspun yarn can make a great embellishment if you know how to use it. Couched embroidery is a beautiful, easy way to attach yarn to a scarf or other accessory for a decorative touch. If you have more yarn, matching fringe is a great way to punch up a plain scarf. This project uses a variegated yarn, but you can substitute several different solid yarns for a more eclectic look. For a soft, cozy project, wool felt is a great choice, but you could take this project in a more elegant direction by using a silk scarf blank instead.

Project Information

YARN
22 yds (20m) coordinating thick-and-thin handspun singles, approx 11 wpi

MATERIALS
6" × 72" (15cm × 183cm) piece of craft felt
clear quilting thread
sewing needle
chalk or quilting pencil
straight pins
scissors
crochet hook

Instructions

Using the provided template (on page 104) or a pattern of your choice, transfer the embroidery pattern to the craft felt with the chalk or the quilting pencil. Pin the pieces of handspun yarn in place along the lines of the embroidery pattern (see Couching on page 104). Whipstitch the yarn to the craft felt with the clear quilting thread, spacing the stitches approximately every ³⁄₁₆" (5mm).

Fold over ¼" (6mm) of felt at each end of the scarf and cut thirty evenly spaced ⅛" (3mm) slits on each end of the scarf for fringe. Cut the remaining handspun yarn into sixty 12" (30cm) pieces for fringe. See Attaching Fringe on page 105 to attach the fringe to both ends of the scarf. Once all of the fringe is attached, trim the ends even.

Couching

Couching is an embroidery technique that uses a thin thread to secure a thick, decorative thread to a fabric, forming a raised pattern; in other words, the perfect way to embroider with handspun yarn. You can spin a yarn specifically for a couched project, or save up all of your handspun scraps for a project made from leftovers. Either way, couching is sure to display your handspun to its advantage.

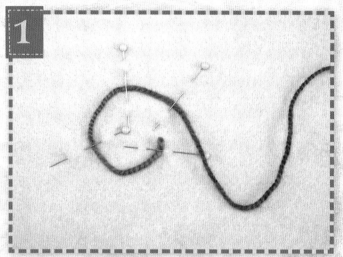

Pin yarn in pattern
Pin pieces of handspun yarn in place along the lines of the embroidery pattern.

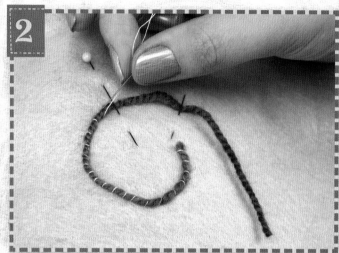

Sew yarn to base
Whipstitch the yarn to the craft felt with thread, spacing the stitches approximately every ³⁄₁₆" (5mm). To hide the couching thread, you can use clear quilting thread or a thread that matches your yarn. You can also choose a contrasting thread for an added decorative element.

Swirl template

Attaching Fringe

Adding fringe is an easy way to liven up any scarf. And fringe is especially great for handspun because it is very forgiving of lumps and bumps. As a matter of fact, the more "interesting" a yarn is, the better! It all adds visual interest to your project. Fringe does take up a lot of yardage, but if you've been bitten by the spinning bug, you probably won't mind spinning a long yarn.

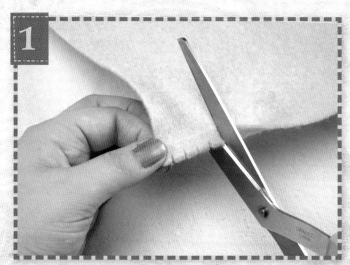

Trim edges
Fold over the edge of your scarf about ¼" (6mm). Cut evenly spaced ⅛" (3mm) slits on the fold.

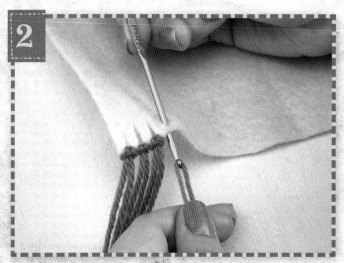

Begin attaching fringe
Cut yarn into pieces for the fringe. Fold a strand of yarn in half, place the crochet hook through a slit in the end of the scarf and pull the looped end of the yarn through the slit.

Finish attaching fringe
Thread the yarn tails through the looped end and then pull the yarn tails to tighten the fringe on the edge of the scarf.

Bubbly Table Runner

This fun project combines two different crafts that use roving: spinning and needle felting. Needle felting doesn't just work on roving—it works on yarn, too. You can spin yarns especially for this table runner in colors to match your dining décor, or you can use up bits of yarn left from other projects. I do recommend sticking with singles yarns for this project, however. You will get tidier lines with singles than you will with plied yarns. Try this table runner to dress up your dining room in a fun, fibery way.

Make It Your Own

Spinning singles can be very rewarding because you can get a good amount of yardage without a lot of effort. There's no spinning a second or third single, and you save the plying time. However, without ply twist to balance the singles twist, singles yarn can be a handful to handle. For instance, using singles for knitting results in an unbalanced fabric. Picking the right project for your singles yarns instead of struggling against their "design features" will help you be a happy crafter.

Project Information

YARN
8 yds (7m) thick-and-thin handspun singles, approx 9 wpi

MATERIALS
felting needle
felting mat
chalk or quilting pencil
iron
¼" (6mm) fusible tape
18" × 54" (46cm × 137cm) piece of craft felt for center
4" × 14½' (10cm × 4.5m) piece of craft felt for border

Instructions

Using the chalk or the quilting pencil, mark the 18" × 54" (46cm × 137cm) piece of craft felt with circles of various sizes. Needle felt the yarn to the craft felt following the pattern lines (see Needle Felting on page 109). Make sure to move the felting mat often to keep the yarn from felting to the mat. Once the needle felting is complete, press the table runner with a steam iron.

Cut the remaining piece of craft felt into two 5' (1.5m) and two 26" (66cm) pieces. Attach the strips to the edges of the runner with fusible tape to form a border.

Needle Felting

Needle felting is a fun and easy way to embellish a project with wool or fiber. A few jabs of the needle (OK, a lot of jabs) and you're done. This is a great way to work out a little frustration or aggression, too! Just be sure to watch your fingers while you're working. Felting needles are sharp!

Begin needle felting
Mark the pattern on the base fabric. You can mark the pattern with the chalk or the quilting pencil, or pin a paper template to the base fabric and work around it, as I'm doing here. Pin or hold the yarn in place on the pattern. Place the needle-felting mat under the base fabric directly under the area where you will be working. Jab the yarn repeatedly with the felting needle to secure it to the base fabric. Occasionally test the yarn to see how secure it is. When a small section of the yarn is securely attached to the base, move on to the next section.

Continue needle felting
Continue working along the pattern, securing the yarn as you go.

Finish needle felting
Secure the yarn along the pattern until you reach the end. Here, because I am working with a circle, I overlap the beginning of the circle with the yarn tail to secure the two ends together.

GALLERY

This book shows you how to get started with spinning, and once you've done that, there's a wide world of spinning ahead of you. Here are some yarns to inspire you as you continue your spinning journey. There's a world of color and texture available in the form of fiber, and a world of choices you can make to shape your yarns. Several talented spinners shared their yarn with me, and I'm happy to show off their beautiful work here and throughout this book to inspire you. Take a look at these lovely yarns and get a glimpse of what the future could hold for you and your spinning.

Beth Sundheim
Chain plied yarn, Romney
wool from Fantom Farm

Cheryl Francis
seedstitch.blogspot.com
3-ply yarn, 2 plies Romney wool and
1 ply mohair from Fantom Farm

Cheryl Francis
seedstitch.blogspot.com
2-ply yarn, 80% merino wool,
20% silk from Sereknitty

Cheryl Francis
seedstitch.blogspot.com
2-ply yarn, superwash merino
wool from Knitterly Things

Tonyia Harkins Little
www.20acresnosheep.net
3-ply yarn, "wool of unknown
parentage" dyed by Tonyia

Tonyia Harkins Little
www.20acresnosheep.net
2-ply yarn, Coopworth wool with bits
of handspun wool carded by Tonyia

Julia Farwell-Clay
www.mothheaven.com and
www.twistcollective.com
2-ply yarn, superwash Merino
wool from Knitterly Things

Janel Laidman
www.janellaidman.com
2-ply yarn, wool with sari silk

115

Susan Markle
www.tradingpostfiber.com
3-ply yarn, Polwarth wool
from Rovings

Susan Markle
www.tradingpostfiber.com
3-ply yarn, blend from
Crosspatch Creations

Susan Markle
www.tradingpostfiber.com
3-ply yarn, blend from
Crosspatch Creations

Susan Markle
www.tradingpostfiber.com
2-ply yarn, blend from
Crosspatch Creations

Susan Markle
www.tradingpostfiber.com
Chain-plied yarn, blend from
Crosspatch Creations

June Oshiro
www.twosheep.com/blog
Singles yarn, Border
Leicester wool

118

June Oshiro
www.twosheep.com/blog
2-ply yarn, 60% Rambouillet
wool, 40% angora

June Oshiro
www.twosheep.com/blog
3-ply yarn, wool, silk and
alpaca blend

119

Kimberly Desko
2-ply yarn, extra-fine Merino
wool dyed by Kim

Cosette Cornelius-Bates
http://cosymakes.com
2-ply yarn, domestic wool
dyed by Cosette

120

Cosette Cornelius-Bates
http://cosymakes.com
Singles yarn, Shetland wool
dyed by Cosette

Jennifer Claydon
assortment of my first yarns

Knitting Resources

Knitting Needle Conversions

diameter (mm)	US size	suggested yarn weight
2	0	Lace Weight
2.25	1	Lace and Fingering Weight
2.75	2	Lace and Fingering Weight
3.25	3	Fingering and Sport Weight
3.5	4	Fingering and Sport Weight
3.75	5	DK and Sport Weight
4	6	DK, Sport and Aran/Worsted Weight
4.5	7	Aran/Worsted Worsted
5	8	Aran/Worsted and Heavy Worsted
5.5	9	Aran/Worsted, Heavy Worsted and Chunky/Bulky
6	10	Chunky/Bulky
6.5	10½	Chunky/Bulky and Super Bulky
8	11	Chunky/Bulky and Super Bulky
9	13	Super Bulky
10	15	Super Bulky
12.75	17	Super Bulky
15	19	Super Bulky
20	36	Super Bulky

Standard Knitting Abbreviations

beg	beginning
BO	bind off
CC	contrast color
CO	cast on
dpn(s)	double-pointed needle(s)
k	knit
k2tog	knit 2 together
MC	main color
p	purl
(in) patt	(in pattern)
pm	place marker
rem	remaining
RS	right side
rep	repeat
rnd	round
St st	Stockinette stitch
st(s)	stitch(es)
tog	together
WS	wrong side

	Super Bulky (6)	Bulky (5)	Medium (4)	Light (3)	Fine (2)	Superfine (1)	Lace (0)
Type	bulky, roving	chunky, craft, rug	worsted, afghan, aran	dk, light worsted	sport, baby	sock, fingering, baby	fingering, 10-count crochet thread
Knit Gauge Range	6–11 sts	12–15 sts	16–20 sts	21–24 sts	23–26 sts	27–32 sts	33–40 sts
Recommended Needle in US Size Range	11 and larger	9 to 11	7 to 9	5 to 7	3 to 5	1 to 3	000 to 1

Yarn Weight Guidelines

Because the names given to different weights of yarn can vary widely depending on the country of origin or the yarn manufacturer's preference, the Craft Yarn Council of America has put together a standard yarn weight system to impose a bit of order on the sometimes unruly yarn labels. Look for a picture of a skein of yarn with a number 0–6 on most kinds of yarn to figure out its "official" weight. Gauge is given over 4" (10cm) of Stockinette stitch. The information in the chart above is taken from www.yarnstandards.com.

Substituting Yarns

If you substitute yarn, be sure to select a yarn of the same weight as the yarn recommended for the project. Even after checking that the recommended gauge on the yarn you plan to substitute is the same as for the yarn listed in the pattern, make sure to knit a swatch to ensure that the yarn and needles you are using will produce the correct gauge.

Glossary

auxiliary – a substance added to a dye bath to aid in dyeing

ball winder – a machine used to wind yarn into a center-pull ball

batt – a sheet of carded fiber

carded – fiber preparation with crossed fibers and shorter fibers that remain mixed in

combed – fiber preparation with parallel fibers and shorter fibers removed

crimp – waves naturally occurring in fibers

draft – to thin out a bundle of fiber by pulling

gauge – a measurement used to describe the stitches and rows per inch in a knitted piece

leader – a length of thread or yarn used to attach fiber to a spinning wheel or spindle

niddy noddy – a tool used to wind yarn into a skein

pencil roving – a thin rope of carded fiber, roughly as thick as a pencil

ply – to join two or more strands of yarn into one, or a strand of yarn in a plied yarn

roving – a rope of carded fibers about as thick as your wrist

selvedge – the right and left edges of woven fabric on the loom

single – a yarn composed of a single unplied strand

skein – yarn organized in a series of layered circles

sliver – a thin rope of carded fiber

top – a rope of combed fibers about as thick as your wrist

warp – the vertical, stationary strands of yarn used in weaving

weft – the horizontal, active strands of yarn used in weaving

whorl – the weight that drives the motion of a spindle or the pulley that drives the flyer on a spinning wheel

woolen – spinning method used to produce fuzzy, airy yarns

worsted – spinning method used to produce smooth, dense yarns

wpi – wraps per inch, a measurement used to classify yarn weight

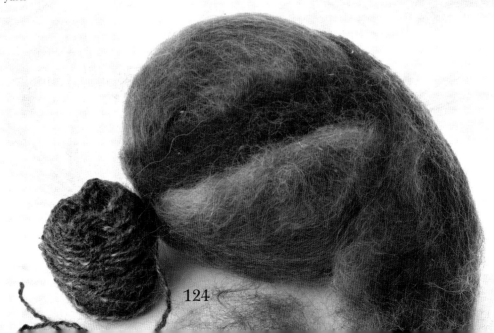

Resources

To become a real spinner, you're going to have to accumulate a spinner's stash of luscious fibers and beautiful tools. Local suppliers are always my first choice, but if you're not lucky enough to have a local resource for fiber goodies or a yearly festival nearby, you can surf the Internet for all manner of fiber finds. These fine vendors will help fill your studio with the best there is in tools, fiber and dyestuff, and the wholesalers listed will have lists of local retailers for you to peruse.

Ashford Wheels & Looms
www.ashford.co.nz
Wholesaler of spinning wheels, spindles, spinning tools, fiber, books, dye

Ashland Bay Trading Company
www.ashlandbay.com
Wholesaler of spinning fibers

Etsy
www.etsy.com
A great place to find spinning fiber and tools from a variety of artists

Louet North America
www.louet.com
Wholesaler of spinning wheels, spindles, spinning tools, fiber, dye

Paradise Fibers
www.paradisefibers.net
Retailer of a wide variety of spinning wheels, spindles, spinning tools, fiber, books, dye, as well as their own line of microblends and painted fibers. A great resource if you aren't able to find something locally.

PRO Chemical & Dye
www.prochemical.com
Dye, auxiliaries, and hard-to-find dyeing tools

Educational resources

In addition to supplies, you might need some more educational resources as your spinning expertise increases. The lessons in this book are merely a starting point for your spinning and dyeing education. Once you've mastered these techniques, expand your fiber world with lessons from some of these talented handspinners. Here are some resources for your spinning education.

Books

Hands On Spinning, Lee Raven, Interweave Press, 1987
Informative primer on spindle and wheel spinning

Teach Yourself Visually Handspinning, Judith MacKenzie McCuin, Wiley Publishing, Inc., 2007
Information-filled, picture-heavy book from one of spinning's foremost teachers

The Alden Amos Big Book of Handspinning, Alden Amos, Interweave Press, 2001
Comprehensive tome of every bit of information you'd ever want to know about spinning

The Twisted Sisters Sock Workbook, Lynne Vogel, Interweave Press, 2002
Spinning and dyeing fiber for socks, socks and more socks

Color in Spinning, Deb Menz, Interweave Press, 1998
Everything you need to know about using Lanaset and Sabraset dyes

Spinning Designer Yarns, Diane Varney, Interweave Press, 2003
For taking your spinning in new directions

Magazines

Spin-Off
www.interweave.com/spin/spinoff_magazine
A magazine with informative articles featuring spinning techniques and projects

Wild Fibers
www.wildfibersmagazine.com
A magazine that provides a fascinating look at spinning around the world

Web sites

Spindlicity
www.spindlicity.com
An online magazine for all spinners, with a focus on spinning with spindles

Knitty
http://knitty.com
Check out the recurring feature, Knittyspin, for spinning patterns and information

The Joy of Handspinning
www.joyofhandspinning.com
A Web site with lots of spinning information and helpful how-to videos

Index

Find More Fiber Inspiration in These North Light Books

KNIT ONE, EMBELLISH TOO

By Cosette Cornelius-Bates

Knit One, Embellish Too features warm and cozy knitted accessories for head, hands and neck, all embellished with embroidery, buttons and appliqués. With a little yarn and a little know how, you can quickly create any of the 35+ projects in this book, and author Cosette Cornelius-Bates helps you with both. Learn how to turn a sweater from a thrift shop into a lovely pile of knitting yarn, and then learn the knitting and embellishing techniques to turn yarn into hats, mittens and scarves for yourself and your loved ones. Get inspired to create your own one-of-a-kind knitted accessories!

ISBN-13: 978-1-60061-046-2

ISBN-10: 1-60061-046-3

paperback with flaps, 128 pages, Z1594

CLOSELY KNIT

By Hannah Fettig

Closely Knit is filled with thoughtful knitted gifts to fit all the people you love: special handknits for mothers, daughters, sisters, the men in your life, precious wee ones and treasured friends. From luxurious scarves and wearable sweaters to cozy socks and even a quick-to-knit heart pin, there really is something for everyone on your list in this book. Projects range from quick and simple to true labors of love, and each is rated with a handy time guide so you can choose what to knit based on how much time you have. Bonus quick-fix options will save the day when you need to whip up a meaningful gift in a jiffy.

ISBN-13: 978-1-60061-018-9

ISBN-10: 1-60061-018-8

paperback with flaps, 144 pages, Z1280

SWEET NEEDLE FELTS

By Jenn Docherty

Sweet Needle Felts features all the techniques and information you will need to begin needle felting, including step-by-step instructions for 25 adorable projects. Learn how to create wearable items such as jewelry, scarves, hats and bags. Decorate your home with cozy pillows and rugs. Needle felt huggable, lovable dolls and toys, including author Jenn Docherty's signature bear. Using just a few simple tools, turn soft, warm wool into colorful creations to wear, give and hug!

ISBN-13: 978-1-60061-039-4

ISBN-10: 1-60061-039-0

paperback, 128 pages, Z1490

These books and other fine North Light books are available at your local bookstore or online supplier. Or visit our Web site, **www.mycraftivity.com**.